THE BIBLE SPEAKS

JAMES M. GRAY

Developed as a study course by Emmaus Correspondence School, founded in 1942.

Many Bible study courses may also be taken via smart phones, tablets, and computers. For more information, visit the ECS website www.ecsministries.org.

The Bible Speaks
James M. Gray, D.D., L.L.D.

Published by:
  Emmaus Correspondence School
  (A division of ECS Ministries)
  P.O. Box 1028
  Dubuque, IA 52004-1028
  phone: (563) 585-2070
  email: ecsorders@ecsministries.org
  website: www.ecsministries.org

First Edition 2015 (AK '15), 1 U<small>NIT</small>

ISBN 978-1-59387-228-1

Code: TBS

Copyright © 2015 ECS Ministries

All rights in this course are reserved. No part of this publication may be reproduced or transmitted in any manner, electronic or mechanical, including photocopy, recording, or any information storage and retrieval system including the Internet without written permission from the publisher. Permission is not needed for brief quotations embodied in critical articles and reviews.

This course was originally published by The Moody Bible Institute of Chicago. *Basic Christian Doctrine* (formerly titled *Scriputre Truth*). The content provides a preliminary series of lessons in systematic Bible study. Dr. Alfred Martin and Dr. Jay Fernlund contributed to the subsequent revision. Copyright © 1965, 1987 by The Moody Bible Institute of Chicago, revised 1993, 1996, 2004. Permission has been given to ECS Ministries to include this course in the ECS Curriculum. This edition has been edited with minor revisions (including changing quoted Scripture passages to the New King James Version) and retitled *The Bible Speaks*.

All Scripture quotations, unless otherwise indicated, are taken from the New King James Version. Copyright © 1979, 1980, 1982 by Thomas Nelson, Inc. Used by permission. All rights reserved.

Printed in the United States of America

STUDENT INSTRUCTIONS

The Bible is God's communication to man, and in that sense we can say that the Bible "speaks" to us. The thinking person who has questions about life, the world, and the future will find answers in the Bible. In this course you will discover first why we can trust the Bible as coming from God, and then some of the main things it says about God and our relationship to Him—in short, the basic teachings of the Christian faith.

LESSONS YOU WILL STUDY

1. What the Bible Says About the Bible 5
2. What the Bible Says About God 11
3. What the Bible Says About the Trinity 19
4. What the Bible Says About God's Relation to the World 25
5. What the Bible Says About Creation and the Fall of Man 31
6. What the Bible Says About Sin 37
7. What the Bible Says About the Person of Christ 43
8. What the Bible Says About the Work of Christ 49
9. What the Bible Says About the Holy Spirit 57
10. What the Bible Says About Faith and Repentance 63
11. What the Bible Says About the Christian's Heritage 68
12. What the Bible Says About Growing as a Christian 76

Course Components

This course has two parts: this study course and the exam booklet.

How To Study

This study has twelve chapters, and each chapter has its own exam. Begin by asking God to help you understand the material. Read the chapter through at least twice, once to get a general idea of its contents and then again, slowly, looking up any Bible references given.

Begin studying immediately, or if you are in a group, as soon as the group begins. We suggest that you keep a regular schedule by trying to complete at least one chapter per week.

Exams

In the exam booklet there is one exam for each chapter (exam 1 covers chapter 1 of the course). Do not answer the questions by what you think or have always believed. The questions are designed to find out if you understand the material given in the course.

After you have completed each chapter, review the related exam and see how well you know the answers. If you find that you are having difficulty answering the questions, review the material until you think you can answer the questions. It is important that you read the Bible passages referenced as some questions may be based on the Bible text.

How Your Exams Are Graded

Your instructor will mark any incorrectly answered questions. You will be referred back to the place in the course where the correct answer is to be found. After finishing this course with a passing average, you will be awarded a certificate.

If you enrolled in a class, submit your exam papers to the leader or secretary of the class who will send them for the entire group to the Correspondence School.

See the back of the exam booklet for more information on returning the exams for grading.

CHAPTER

1

What the Bible Says About the Bible

Various names are used for the Bible, such as *The Holy Bible*, *The Scriptures*, and *The Word of God*. The word *Bible* comes from a Greek word which originally meant "books," but through a gradual change of usage the word came to be regarded as a singular "book." To call the Bible a "book" is very appropriate, for beyond question the Bible is *the* Book.

The Bible is called *holy* because of its sacred character as coming from God. The term *scriptures* mean "writings." This is the term most often used in the Bible in reference to itself, occurring about fifty times (including both the singular and the plural forms). Paul, in writing to Timothy, used the expression, "the Holy Scriptures" (2 Timothy 3:15).

The Bible is divided into two parts: the Old Testament and the New Testament. The Old Testament has thirty-nine books and is the record of God's dealings with man—especially with the nation of Israel, God's "chosen" people—before Jesus Christ was born; it also includes prophecies about Christ's coming. The New Testament contains twenty-seven books, the first four of which tell about the life, death, and resurrection of Christ. The rest of the New Testament proclaims the salvation that God offers in light of Christ's coming.

The Bible Is Inspired of God

"All Scripture is given by inspiration of God, and is profitable for doctrine, for reproof, for correction, for instruction in righteousness, that the man of God may be complete, thoroughly equipped for every good work" (2 Timothy 3:16-17).

The phrase "by inspiration" is literally, "God-breathed." Nothing is closer to a living being than its breath; the Bible comes direct from God. The Bible is inspired by God in the sense that (a) it is *His* communication, and (b) He is the ultimate Author behind the men who penned it.

1. God Spoke It

David said, "The Spirit of the LORD spoke by me, and His word was on my tongue" (2 Samuel 23:2).

The LORD told Jeremiah, "Behold, I have put My words in your mouth" (Jeremiah 1:9).

The prophets said again and again, "This is what the Sovereign LORD says . . ." (e.g., Ezekiel 5:5).

In the New Testament, the apostle Paul wrote to the Thessalonian church that "when you received the word [in this context, the message of the gospel] of God which you heard from us, you welcomed it not as the word of men, but as it is in truth, the word of God, which also effectively works in you who believe" (1 Thessalonians 2:13).

2. God Caused Men to Write It in His Name

Some people maintain that the Bible only *contains* the word of God, thereby setting themselves up as judges to determine what in the Bible is inspired and what is not. On the contrary, the truth is that the Bible *is* the word of God. The Bible originated from God. He directed the men He had chosen to write down exactly what He wanted written.

> *"For prophecy never came by the will of man, but holy men of God spoke as they were moved by the Holy Spirit" (2 Peter 1:21).*

The word "moved" in this verse is used in Greek to describe the moving of a ship by the wind towards its planned destination; Bible writers were "borne along" by the Spirit to write what God designed to accomplish with those words and wording.

Since thoughts cannot be divorced from words, the very words and order of them in the original Scriptures were given by God, as Paul tells us in 1 Corinthians 2:13, "These things we also speak, not in words which man's wisdom teaches but which the Holy Spirit teaches, comparing spiritual things with spiritual." This doctrine is called *verbal inspiration*. The term *plenary inspiration* means that all parts of the Bible are equally authoritative owing to it all originating from God. The Bible declares this to be a fact without telling us exactly how God did it. In some way, mysterious to us, He influenced the writers of Scripture to record His message to mankind. God worked through these men in such a way that their personalities are evident—for instance, John did not write in the same style as Paul, yet what each of them wrote is the inspired word of God.

The Bible Is the Revelation of God

Revelation is God's act of making known to us those things that we otherwise could never know. Men always have sought to discover the truth concerning their Creator and His relationship to the world, but the things of God cannot be found by ordinary human means.

> *"But as it is written: 'Eye has not seen, nor ear heard, nor have entered into the heart of man the things which God has prepared for those who love Him.' But God has revealed them to us by His Spirit" (1 Corinthians 2:9-10).*

The Bible is both a revelation *from* God and a revelation *of* God in that it comes from God and tells us about Him. This revelation is twofold:

1. God Reveals Himself in His Written Word

> *"I am the LORD, and there is no other. I have not spoken in secret, in a dark place of the earth; I not say to the seed of Jacob, 'Seek Me in vain'; I the LORD speak righteousness, I declare things that are right" (Isaiah 45:18-19).*

Every page of Scripture reveals the person, work, and purposes of God. The very first verse tells us three things about Him: (1) He existed before the universe did; (2) He created everything; (3) by inference, He is all-powerful (Genesis 1:1). Some information has to be gleaned with deeper study, as when the resurrected Christ talked with two of His disciples on the road to Emmaus:

> *"And beginning at Moses and all the Prophets, He [Jesus] explained to them in all the Scriptures the things concerning Himself" (Luke 24:27). See also Luke 1:1-4; 24:44; John 5:39-47; and Acts 1:1-2.*

2. God Reveals Himself in His Son, Jesus Christ, Who Is the Living Word

> *"In the beginning was the Word, and the Word was with God, and the Word was God. . . . And the Word became flesh and dwelt among us, and we beheld His glory, the glory as of the only begotten of the Father, full of grace and truth" (John 1:1, 14).*

> *"God, who at various times and in various ways spoke in time past to the fathers by the prophets, has in these last days spoken to us by His Son . . ." (Hebrews 1:1-2).*

The Bible Is Trustworthy

Because the Author of the Bible is the infallible God, we can logically say that the Bible is the only infallible rule of faith and practice. It bears testimony of itself:

> *"Forever, O LORD, Your word is settled in heaven" (Psalm 119:89).*

Someone has said, "If a man lies to me once, I wouldn't know when to trust him if he told me the truth a thousand times." The Bible does not lie to us even once. We can have confidence that what it says regarding spiritual things is true because what it says about history and science is true (though it is neither a history book nor a science book). Consider the following example (one of many). Ancient historians said Nabonidus was king of Babylon at the time of its fall to the Persians in 539 BC. The Bible, however, states that Belshazzar was king at that time. Was the Bible wrong? No. Archeologists have since uncovered tablets in Babylon showing that Belshazzar was co-ruler with his father, Nabonidus. Thus we see a historical account in the Bible that has been shown to be true.

The Bible Is God's Message to Man

Since the Bible is our guidebook for life, and since our conduct is to be governed in all things by what the Scriptures teach, let us examine those particular things in it and give them our undivided attention. These particulars can be summarized briefly in a threefold way:

1. God's Only Plan of Salvation from Sin

The Scriptures teach what God has done to provide salvation for mankind. We will look deeper into God's plan of salvation in another lesson; our purpose now is to simply know that this great truth is taught in the Bible. Some people try to work for their salvation through various ways and means, but God reveals to us in His Word the only way to be made right with Him: believe in the gospel of Jesus Christ.

> *"I am not ashamed of the gospel, for it is the power of God to salvation for everyone who believes, for the Jew first and also for the Greek [Gentile]" (Romans 1:16).*

> *". . . And that from childhood you have known the Holy Scriptures, which are able to make you wise for salvation through faith which is in Christ Jesus" (2 Timothy 3:15).*

2. Man's Responsibility to Receive God's Salvation

The Scriptures teach what we must each do personally in order to experience this salvation—that is, they teach what we must do in order to be saved from being punished eternally for our sin against God. We might possibly know about the love and mercy of God even without the Bible, but the only way to know how to be saved is found in the Bible.

> *"Believe on the Lord Jesus Christ, and you will be saved" (Acts 16:31).*

> *"For God so loved the world that He gave His only begotten Son, that whoever believes in Him should not perish but have everlasting life" (John 3:16).*

> *"But as many as received Him, to them He gave the right to become children of God, to those who believe in His name" (John 1:12).*

Just as a person accepts a gift from a friend with no thought of paying for it, so we receive the blessings of life in Christ without exchanging any payment for them.

3. Man's Condition in the Life to Come

The Scriptures teach about the future life (Revelation 21:1-8).

> *"Now I saw a new heaven and a new earth, for the first heaven and the first earth had passed away. Also there was no more sea. Then I, John, saw the holy city, New Jerusalem, coming down out of heaven from God, prepared as a bride adorned for her husband. And I heard a loud voice from heaven saying, 'Behold, the tabernacle of God is with men, and He will dwell with them, and they shall be His people. God Himself will be with them and be their God. And God will wipe away every tear from their eyes; there shall be no more death, nor sorrow, nor crying. There shall be no more pain, for the former things have passed away.' Then He who sat on the throne said, 'Behold, I make all things new.' And He said to me, 'Write, for these words are true and faithful.' And He said to me, 'It is done! I am the Alpha and the Omega, the Beginning and the End. I will give of the fountain of the water of life freely to him who thirsts. He who overcomes shall inherit all things, and I will be his God and he shall be My son'"*

In every age, people have tried earnestly to find out something about conditions in the life to come without the aid of the Bible. They have tried fortune-telling, and they have tried to talk with the dead. Isaiah 8:19 and Luke 16:29-31 reveal how foolish these attempts are. In contrast to the doubts, uncertainty, and despair of men, the Bible gives us a true and sure message about the life to come.

We have the most wonderful message of all time and of all eternity. The Bible is indeed the Word of God, and in it the God of heaven has told us about Himself and about our relationship to Him. What study could be more valuable than the study of the Bible?

CHAPTER

2

WHAT THE BIBLE SAYS ABOUT GOD

Look at the stars some night when the sky is clear. The Milky Way, stretching across the heavens, is a galaxy containing about 100 billion stars. Since scientists know of the existence of ten billion galaxies like ours, it has been estimated that there are about as many stars in the sky as there are grains of sand on all the seashores on earth!

The psalmist says, "By the word of the LORD the heavens were made . . . For He spoke, and it was done . . ." (Psalm 33:6, 9). This is the God revealed in the Bible. The Bible does not try to prove the existence of God. Rather, it assumes it, revealing Him in the following ways:

"God Is a Spirit" (John 4:24)

Most people find it difficult to think of reality apart from material things. All about us are things that we can see and touch. But God, who is the greatest reality of all, cannot be seen or touched, because He is a spirit being.

The Bible speaks of God as "the invisible God" (Colossians 1:15). From the words of the Lord Jesus in Luke 24:39 it is clear that a spirit does not have bodily form. No one has ever seen a pure spirit—that is, a spirit without some outward form. The fact that God is a spirit involves the additional fact that He is a personal Being who knows and thinks and acts. He is not some merely vague, impersonal force. When the Bible says that man was made in God's image (Genesis 1:26), it means that man is a thinking creature who has feelings and a will, just as his Creator does.

In His Being, God Is:

1. Infinite

God is different from every other spirit being in that He is infinite. Any other spirits that exist are created by Him and are all finite, or limited. God is not limited or confined in any way.

> *"I am God, and there is no other; I am God, and there is none like Me, declaring the end from the beginning, and from ancient times things that are not yet done, saying, 'My counsel shall stand, and I will do all My pleasure'" (Isaiah 46:9-10).*

2. Eternal

The word *eternal* means more than "endless." Something may be endless, but it did once have a beginning. God, however, had no beginning and He will have no end. God Himself was not made or caused by anyone or anything. He has eternal self-existence.

> *"Even from everlasting to everlasting, You are God" (Psalm 90:2).*

> *"'I am the Alpha and the Omega' says the Lord God, 'who is, and who was, and who is to come, the Almighty'" (Revelaton 1:8).*

3. Unchangeable

God does not change. What He always has been, He is now and always will be. Change is characteristic of finite beings and things. The infinite, eternal God is always the same, immutable (unchangeable) in His absolute perfection.

> *"I the LORD do not change" (Malachi 3:6).* See also Hebrews 13:8 and James 1:17.

> *"God is not a man, that He should lie, nor a son of man, that He should repent. Has He said, and will He not do? Or has He spoken, and will He not make it good?" (Numbers 23:19)*

The Attributes of God

What we call the *attributes of God* are the qualities of His being that determine His activity; they are those things that are characteristic of God. There is no easy way to classify these attributes, although some students of the Bible divide them into two categories: His natural attributes and His moral attributes.

God's *natural attributes* are those that are true of God alone and cannot be passed on to any creature. His *moral attributes* are qualities that God has in absolute perfection but which, in a relative sense, are possible for man to evidence as well.

1. God's Natural Attributes

a. Omniscience

God has complete and perfect knowledge of all things in the past, present, and future. God has perfect knowledge of all things because He is omniscient. God exercises this perfect knowledge in a perfect manner for His own glory and for the good of His creation. This is infinite wisdom. Speaking rhetorically, the prophet Isaiah asked,

> *"Who has directed the Spirit of the LORD, or who as His counselor has taught Him, and taught Him in the path of justice? Who taught Him knowledge, and showed Him the way of understanding?" (Isaiah 40:13-14)*

> *"Oh, the depth of the riches of both the wisdom and knowledge of God! How unsearchable are His judgments and His ways past finding out!" (Romans 11:33).*

b. Omnipotence

God is able to do anything that He wills to do. His power is unlimited; He is "Almighty God" (Genesis 17:1). This attribute is called omnipotence. The God who created the universe out of nothing can do anything.

> *"By the word of the LORD the heavens were made, and all the host of them by the breath of His mouth. . . . Let the earth fear the LORD . . . for He spoke, and it was done; He commanded, and it stood fast" (Psalm 33:6, 8-9).*

Naturally, God cannot do anything that would involve sin or absurdity, for that would be out of harmony with His nature. However, this is not a limitation of His power; it is, instead, an affirmation of it. For instance, when the Bible says that God "cannot lie" (Titus 1:2), it is not putting a limit upon His omnipotence—rather, it affirms His complete truthfulness. See Psalm 62:11; Ephesians 3:20-21; and Matthew 28:18 for other references on this subject.

c. Omnipresence

God is present everywhere at once in the fullness of His being. We cannot understand this fully, and we must avoid thinking of God as if He were some kind of rare material substance stretching to every part of the universe and divisible into many parts. Since God is an infinite Spirit, He is personally present everywhere. See 1 Kings 8:27 and Psalm 139:7-12.

2. His Moral Attributes

Morality has to do with standards of perfection. God Himself sets these standards and displays them in His character and conduct. A good summary verse for God's moral attributes is Exodus 34:6-7, spoken by God, describing Himself to Moses:

> *"The LORD, the LORD God, merciful and gracious, longsuffering and abounding in goodness and truth, keeping mercy for thousands, forgiving iniquity and sin by no means clearing the gulity, visiting the iniquity of the fathers upon the children and the children's children to the third and fourth generation."*

a. Holiness

Holiness is that perfection in God in which He eternally wills and maintains His own moral excellence. His holiness regulates the perfect harmony of all His attributes. Throughout the Bible, God is described as holy; in the book of Isaiah alone God is called "the Holy One of Israel" twenty-five times.

The heavenly hosts praise Him in these words: "Holy, holy, holy is the Lord God Almighty, who was, and is, and is to come" (Revelation 4:8).

The word *holy* is difficult to define. Negatively, it means that God is absolutely separate from all evil and from all that would defile. Positively, it asserts His absolute moral purity and rightness. "God is light and in Him is no darkness at all" (1 John 1:5).

b. Justice

The term *justice* is used interchangeably in the Scripture with the word *righteousness*. Since God is pure and holy in all He is, He naturally is perfectly right or just in all He does. He manifests His righteousness in His hatred of sin and His love of things done right.

> *"The LORD . . . will do no unrighteousness. Every morning He brings His justice to light; He never fails" (Zephaniah 3:5).*

God's righteousness and holiness demand that He punish sinners:

> *"He has appointed a day on which He will judge the world in righteousness by the Man whom He has ordained. He has given assurance of this to all by raising Him from the dead." (Acts 17:31)* See also Psalm 9:78; Revelation 6:10.

c. Goodness

The Lord Jesus once remarked to a young man that only God is absolutely good (Matthew 19:17). This word may be thought by some to equate to holiness, but it conveys primarily the thought of God's benevolence—the exercise of mercy or loving kindness toward His creation.

> *"You are good, and do good" (Psalm 119:68).*

> *"The LORD is good to all, and His tender mercies are over all His works" (Psalm 145:9).*

d. Love

> *"God is love" (1 John 4:8).*

Out of God's essential nature of love flow His grace, mercy, and kindness. The love of God is His moral determination to give of Himself for the good of others; it was His delight in (and desire for) the welfare of His creatures that caused Him to manifest Himself in the person and work of His Son, the Lord Jesus Christ.

> *"In this the love of God was manifested toward us, that God has sent His only begotten Son into the world, that we might live through Him"* (1 John 4:9).

> *"But God demonstrates His own love toward us in that while we were still sinners, Christ died for us"* (Romans 5:8)

In God's holiness His love operates in perfect harmony with all His other attributes (as shown in Exodus 34:6-7 above). At the cross of Christ, for instance, God's justice was satisfied because the penalty for sin was paid. At the same time, God demonstrated grace and love by providing forgiveness for all who believe (Romans 3:24-26).

e. Truth

In God, truth, or veracity, is that which operates in perfect harmony with reality. God cannot lie. He is true in all His ways. This attribute involves also God's faithfulness in fulfilling all His promises—He is "true to His word." Here is an example:

> *"I will worship . . . and praise Your name for Your lovingkindness and Your truth, for You have magnified Your word [promise] above all Your name. In the day when I cried out, You answered me, and made me bold with strength in my soul"* (Psalm 138:2-3).

> *"A God of truth and without injustice; righteous and upright is He"* (Deuteronomy 32:4).

Let us remember that God's holiness, justice, goodness, love, and truth are just as infinite, eternal, and unchangeable as He is; they are all qualities of His Being.

The Only True and Living God

1. There Is But One God

A little boy was once asked how he knew there was only one God. He replied, "Because there's room for only one—He fills heaven and earth." We have already seen that God is infinite, so the boy was right.

> *"There is no other God but one"* (1 Corinthians 8:4).

"Hear, O Israel: The LORD our God, the LORD is one!"
(Deuteronomy 6:4). See also Isaiah 44:8; James 2:19; and
1 Timothy 2:5.

2. This God Is the True God

The word *true* is used here in the sense of real or genuine. God is called "true" to distinguish Him from the idols and false gods that people of all cultures and eras have worshiped. In the West, we do not worship carved images, but rather idols like money, materialism, sports, and prestige. Any so-called god who is different from the God presented in the Bible is worthless. Read Isaiah 46:5-7; 2 Kings 19:17-18; and Acts 14:11-15. This fact ought to motivate us to respect, fear, trust, glorify, love, and obey God.

"Who is like You, O LORD, among the gods, Who is like You, glorious in holiness, fearful in praises, doing wonders?"
(Exodus 15:11)

3. This God Is the Living God

"The LORD lives! Blessed be my Rock! Let the God of my salvation be exalted" (Psalm 18:46).

a. Natural Life

Being the only true and living God, He is also the only *source* of life. God created Adam a "living being" (Genesis 2:7). The life that we enjoy comes from God. We should thank Him for every breath we draw.

"In Him [God] we live and move and have our being" (Acts 17:28).

b. Spiritual Life

Because God is an eternal spirit Being, the life we enter into in relationship to Him is also in the spiritual realm, which is eternal and not related to this world that is passing away.

"The gift of God is eternal life in Christ Jesus our Lord"
(Romans 6:23). See also Romans 8:10; Ephesians 2:4-5; and John 10:27-28.

"And this is eternal life: that they may know You, the only true God, and Jesus Christ, whom You have sent" (John 17:3).

CHAPTER

3

WHAT THE BIBLE SAYS ABOUT THE TRINITY

The Godhead—Father, Son, and Holy Spirit

In our last lesson we saw that the Bible teaches there is only one God. In this lesson we will learn that the one God eternally exists in three persons—Father, Son, and Holy Spirit. This is called the doctrine of the *Trinity*.

Although the word "Trinity" is not in the Bible, it expresses a biblical truth; in fact, it was first used by a writer in the early church to set forth the truth that God is a Tri-unity of persons. The term *Godhead* (or Godhood) refers to God's essence or divine being. It is a proper statement of truth to say that there are three persons in the Godhead.

The Old Testament emphasizes the unity of God—that is, it asserts there is one God in contrast to the many false gods of the heathen. Nevertheless, the Old Testament indicates that God exists in a plurality of persons. For example, the summary word for God (*Elohim*) is a Hebrew plural word: the Spirit of God is mentioned in Genesis 1:2; the Son is mentioned in Psalm 2:7, 12; and there are plural pronouns in a number of places which show that God is a Trinity. When He created man, God said, "Let Us make man in Our image . . ." (Genesis 1:26; see also Isaiah 6:8). If there were only one person in the Godhead, does it not seem unlikely that God would use the words *us* and *our* in this instance? Would He not have been more likely to say, "*I* will make man in *My* image"? See also Genesis 3:22.

The New Testament, while fully recognizing the unity of God, also conveys the fact that He exists in three persons: the Father as God—"For through Him [Jesus] we both have access by one Spirit to the Father" (Ephesians 2:18), the Son as God—"Let this mind be in you which was also in Christ Jesus, who, being in the form of God, did not consider it robbery to be equal with God" (Philippians 2:5-6; see also John 1:1), and the Holy Spirit as God—"But Peter said, 'Ananias, why has Satan filled your heart to lie to the Holy Spirit and keep back part of the price of the land for yourself? While it remained, was it not your own? And after it was sold, was it not in your own control? Why have you conceived this thing in your heart? You have not lied to men but to God'" (Acts 5:3-4). Yet these are not three Gods, but one and the same God in being, essence, and power.

It is difficult, if not impossible, to explain what the word *person* means as applied to the Father, the Son, and the Holy Spirit. We are accustomed to think of persons as individual human beings, and we know that three persons cannot be one being. The persons of the Godhead are clearly distinguished from one another in many passages of Scripture, yet they cannot be separated. This truth is beyond the capacity of our finite minds to fully grasp.

No illustration of the Trinity will sufficiently explain this relationship, but we can perhaps get some help by trying to express the relationship mathematically. We would usually say, one *plus* one *plus* one equals *three*. But of God it would be more accurate to say, one *times* one *times* one equals *one*, for each of the persons in the Godhead is fully God in the absolute sense, and the three together are the one self-same God. It is not possible for us to fully explain this truth, but we can still know and state clearly what the Bible actually says on the subject.

Further Bible Evidence of the Trinity

Consider further testimony from within Scripture that each of the persons is individually called God:

1. Comparing Scripture with Scripture

The passage in Isaiah 6; "Also I heard the voice of the Lord, saying: 'Whom shall I send, and who will go for Us?' Then I said, 'Here am I! Send me'" mentioned previously is even more interesting and presents a stronger proof of the Trinity when compared with John 12:35-41:

> "Then Jesus said to them, 'A little while longer the light is with you. Walk while you have the light, lest darkness overtake you; he who walks in darkness does not know where he is going. While you have the light, believe in the light, that you may become sons of light.' These things Jesus spoke, and departed, and was hidden from them. But although He had done so many signs before them, they did not believe in Him, that the word of Isaiah the prophet might be fulfilled, which he spoke: 'Lord, who has believed our report? And to whom has the arm of the LORD been revealed?' Therefore they could not believe, because Isaiah said again: 'He has blinded their eyes and hardened their hearts, Lest they should see with their eyes, Lest they should understand with their hearts and turn, So that I should heal them.' These things Isaiah said when he saw His glory and spoke of Him."

And Acts 28:25-27:

> So when they did not agree among themselves, they departed after Paul had said one word: "The Holy Spirit spoke rightly through Isaiah the prophet to our fathers, saying, 'Go to this people and say: Hearing you will hear, and shall not understand; And seeing you will see, and not perceive; For the hearts of this people have grown dull. Their ears are hard of hearing, And their eyes they have closed, Lest they should see with their eyes and hear with their ears, Lest they should understand with their hearts and turn, So that I should heal them.'"

In John 12:35-36, in the days before Christ was betrayed and crucified, Jesus was urging His hearers to pay attention to the "light" that was shining among them—speaking of Himself. John records in verse 37 that the people to whom He spoke did not believe in Him, even though He had performed many miracles before them. Then in the following verses, John quotes Isaiah 53:1 and Isaiah 6:10 (written about 700 years before Christ was born), stating Isaiah had foretold that some people would reject their Redeemer because they would harden their hearts against Him. John says plainly that the God whom Isaiah saw was the Lord Jesus: "These things Isaiah said when he saw His glory [implying, in the context, Jesus] and spoke of Him" (John 12:41).

In Acts 28:23, Paul was speaking to the people about Christ, but some of them did not believe in Him. In Acts 28:25-27, Isaiah 6:8-10 is again referred to—this time, as the voice of the Holy Spirit (Acts 28:25).

So we see how this one passage from Isaiah in the Old Testament, when compared with these two New Testament references, brings out the truth that there are three persons in one Godhead.

2. The Manifestation of the Trinity at the Baptism of Jesus

"When He had been baptized, Jesus came up immediately from the water; and behold, the heavens were opened to Him, and He saw the Spirit of God descending like a dove and alighting upon Him. And suddenly a voice came from heaven, saying, 'This is My beloved Son, in whom I am well pleased.'" (Matthew 3:16-17)

Our next evidence can be found in Matthew 3:16-17. Here we have a beautiful picture painted for us as well as additional proof of the Trinity. Here we see Jesus standing in the water, having been baptized by John. And now, behold, the heavens open and the Spirit of God descends like a dove upon Jesus. But wait! A voice is heard from heaven, the voice of the Father, saying, "This is My beloved Son!"

What clearer and better proof can we have than this, that in the Godhead there are three persons—Father, Son, and Holy Spirit?

3. Christ's Declaration Regarding the Trinity in His Great Commission to His Disciples

"Go therefore and make disciples of all the nations, baptizing them in the name of the Father and of the Son and of the Holy Spirit" (Matthew 28:19).

If these three were not God, it would not seem right to give each the same dignity and honor. And if they were more than one God, would not Jesus have been likely to say "in the names" instead of only "in the name"?

4. Paul's Statement in an Apostolic Benediction

"The grace of the Lord Jesus Christ, and the love of God, and the communion of the Holy Spirit be with you all" (2 Corinthians 13:14).

If these three were not equally God, would it be right to give each of them the same importance? Indeed, would it not be an insult to the true God to do this? While there several other similar passages, these are enough for our purpose here.

5. Activities of the Persons of the Godhead

An overview of Scripture reveals that the activities of each person of the Godhead generally fall into particular categories: the Father generates (initiates) and operates; the Son creates and redeems; and the Spirit ministers and produces.

Faith Believes What Cannot Be Understood Intellectually

> *"Now faith is the substance of things hoped for, the evidence of things not seen" (Hebrews 11:1).*

Perhaps after reading and thinking about these statements of the Scripture regarding the Trinity you are ready to exclaim, "This is a great mystery; I cannot understand it!" Don't worry; this is what many other people say. God does not expect us to understand it; God calls us only to believe it on the testimony of His own written Word.

There are a many things in the Bible that we believe but don't understand. For example, we believe that God created the earth and everything in it, but we do not understand how He did it. Neither do we understand why a little brown seed planted in the black soil pushes a little green shoot up through the ground and brings forth a red flower—yet we believe it.

Consider this question: Can you put the whole of the Atlantic Ocean in a teacup? No more can you expect to put the whole of the idea of God into a human brain.

> *"Can you search out the deep things of God? Can you find out the limits of the Almighty? They are higher than heaven—what can you do? Deeper than Sheol [the grave]—what can you know? Their measure is longer than the earth and broader than the sea" (Job 11:7-9).*

> *"Oh, the depth of the riches both of the wisdom and knowledge of God! How unsearchable are His judgments and His paths past finding out!" (Romans 11:33)*

CHAPTER

4

WHAT THE BIBLE SAYS ABOUT GOD'S RELATION TO THE WORLD

People have always asked questions concerning the world in which they live. Here are four of the most important questions asked:

- ➤ Where did the world come from?
- ➤ What holds the world together and keeps it going?
- ➤ Is there any order or government in the world?
- ➤ Is there purpose in the world?

Human philosophies cannot answer these questions, but the Bible does, showing that in every case the answer is *God*.

The Issue of Origin—God the Creator

Where did the universe come from? The Bible tells us plainly in its opening sentence: "In the beginning God created the heavens and the earth" (Genesis 1:1). The phrase "heavens and the earth" means the universe—all that exists apart from God Himself.

The answer, then, to the question of origin is that there is an almighty Creator who called into existence that which did not exist previously.

> *"By faith we understand that the worlds were framed by the word of God's command, so that the things which are seen were not made of things which are visible" (Hebrews 11:3).*

This biblical teaching is in contrast and contradiction to the false theory of evolution, which is popular in the world today but really has no answer to the issue of beginning or origin. The evolutionist believes that matter always has existed in some form; he will not admit to the existence of a Creator. He traces the present life forms back to earlier forms but never actually explains how there came to be matter in the first place. He believes that, by chance, both male and female of a species spontaneously appeared. He ridicules the Christian's faith in God and puts his faith in evolution.

But which is more reasonable: to believe that all things were created by an infinite, eternal, omnipotent God, or to believe that matter has always existed? The Bible declares that God created everything by His powerful word.

> *"By the word of the LORD the heavens were made, and all the host of them by the breath of His mouth . . . For He spoke, and it was done; He commanded, and it stood fast" (Psalm 33:6, 9).*

It is interesting to note that Christ is called the Word of God and that the New Testament speaks of Him as the Creator:

> *"All things were made through Him [the Word, v. 1], and without Him nothing was made that was made" (John 1:3).* See also Colossians 1:15-16 and Hebrews 1:2.

Because the world came from the creative hand of God, it was very good (Genesis 1:31). Sin came in afterward. All the evil we have ever seen or known or heard about in this world is the effect of sin.

The Issue of Preservation—God the Sustainer

God not only made the world, He holds it together and keeps all things working in it. He did not create it and then throw it into space, leaving it to take care of itself the best way it could. Just as it is illogical to think that the universe created itself, it is unreasonable to think that it can sustain itself. Isaiah 40:6-31 tells us about God as the Sustainer. The New Testament shows that, as in creation, Christ's hand is present in preservation.

> *"In Him [Christ] all things consist" (Colossians 1:17).*

> *". . . upholding all things by the word of His [Christ's] power" (Hebrews 1:3).*

The Issue of Direction—God the Governor

Many unbelievers maintain that there is only accident or chance in the world. Here, as in so many other instances, the devil has blinded peoples' minds. Is it easier to believe that this complicated universe proceeds by blind chance, or that the almighty, all-wise God rules it and gives it direction?

Scripture tells us clearly that God is the sovereign Ruler of the universe. "The LORD has established His throne in heaven, and His kingdom rules over all" (Psalm 103:19).

We see in Genesis 3:1-19 the ruling hand of God in relationship to people, to Satan, and to the earth. Man's responsibility under the authority of God is plainly set forth. In Genesis 6 the history of how human wickedness developed, and the consequent judgment of God in the worldwide flood revealed the sovereign hand of God. God's commands to Noah in Genesis 9 also show His sovereignty. The prophet Daniel declared God's rulership of the world and its affairs:

> "Then the secret was revealed to Daniel in a night vision. So Daniel blessed the God of heaven. Daniel answered and said: 'Blessed be the name of God forever and ever, For wisdom and might are His. And He changes the times and the seasons; He removes kings and raises up kings; He gives wisdom to the wise And knowledge to those who have understanding. He reveals deep and secret things; He knows what is in the darkness, And light dwells with Him'" (Daniel 2:19-22). See also Ecclesiastes 11:9; 12:14 and Romans 14:11-12.

Since God has made us, He has the right to set the rules by which we should live and to determine our destiny. To reconcile this with the Bible's teaching that man has a free will is beyond the capability of our finite minds. The Bible says, "The secret things belong to the LORD our God, but those things which are revealed belong to us and to our children forever . . ." (Deuteronomy 29:29). The relationship between God's sovereignty and man's free will is one of God's "secret things."

> "But indeed, O man, who are you to reply against God? Will the thing formed say to him who formed it, 'Why have you made me like this?' Does not the potter have power over the clay, from the same lump to make one vessel for honor and another for dishonor?'" (Romans 9:20-21).

This is not a cause for terror to the one who knows and trusts God; instead it is a cause for rejoicing, for we know that the sovereign Ruler of the universe is the One whose character is perfectly balanced in justice and love. And because God made us and all the rest of the world, we need not fear the power of any creature.

> "The angel of the LORD encamps all around those who fear Him, and He delivers them" (Psalm 34:7).

> "For the eyes of the LORD run to and fro throughout the whole earth to show Himself strong on behalf of those whose heart is loyal to Him" (2 Chronicles 16:9).

> "Look at the birds of the air, for they neither sow nor reap nor gather into barns; yet your heavenly Father feeds them. Are you not of more value than they?" (Matthew 6:26). Also compare Luke 12:6-7.

From all this we may learn how comprehensive is God's care and provision for those who trust themselves to Him.

The Issue of Purpose or Goal—God the Savior

Is there purpose in the universe? Is there a goal toward which all of creation is moving? One place in Scripture we see an answer to this question is in 2 Peter 3:1-15. There we find that God is not only the Creator, Preserver, and Governor of the universe, but also its Deliverer.

Because sin has corrupted the universe, God is working out His plan to deliver the universe from the bondage of corruption and to create ". . . new heavens and a new earth in which righteousness dwells" (2 Peter 3:13). At that time, the universe will be delivered from the sorrow and sighing which now beset it.

> "Then I saw a new heaven and a new earth . . ." (Revelation 21:1). See also Colossians 1:16-20.

> "The creation itself also will be delivered from the bondage of corruption into the glorious liberty of the children of God. For we know that the whole creation groans and labors with birthpangs together until now" (Romans 8:21-22).

We must understand that not all men will be saved, for the Bible is very clear about that, as very few are willing to acknowledge they are sinners in need of a Savior. Personal salvation is only appropriated through faith in the Lord Jesus Christ, and the deliverance of the material universe from the bondage of sin will come only through Him.

This lesson has been a brief glance at the relationship between God and the world. It stands in sharp contrast to human philosophies, which either would separate the universe from God altogether or would make God and the universe identical.

The Bible gives the only satisfactory solution to these ever-recurring questions—the question of origin, the question of preservation, the question of direction, and the question of purpose.

Let's Sum Up

The Bible does not divorce belief from behavior. The more you know, the more you are responsible to apply what you learn to your life. How are you applying the truths you have learned in Lessons 1–4? Below is a capsule summary of the truths taught with each lesson, followed in each case with a statement for you to consider. Do you agree or disagree? Test yourself to see how much this course is really meaning to you.

Lesson 1—The Bible is God's Word: I believe it and aspire to obey it.

Lesson 2—God is not only loving and great, He is also holy: I have experienced God's love for me personally and I realize that He looks with disfavor upon my sin.

Lesson 3—God is a triune God—Father, Son, and Holy Spirit: Only this great incomprehensible God can fill my deepest needs.

Lesson 4—God not only created this world; He is its rightful Ruler: I am willing to give God His rightful place in my life.

If these statements echo your own mind and heart, you are applying the truths to your life and they will be a blessing to you.

CHAPTER

5

What the Bible Says About Creation and the Fall of Man

To advertise its product, a certain paint company illustrated what its paint could do by showing "before and after" pictures. They demonstrate how their paint can transform a drab, unattractive room into one that is bright and cheerful.

In this lesson, the picture is reversed. Here we will see the brightness of man when he came from the hand of God contrasted with the darkness that followed when he listened to Satan.

"God created man in His own image" (Genesis 1:26-27)

We have seen that God is a moral, personal Being. When the Bible declares that God made man in His image, it is conveying that man is a moral being who is responsible to His Creator when it comes to standards of morality. He is a personal being, having intellect, feelings, and will. You and I are personal beings. You are conscious of yourself as an individual and are distinct from all other individuals. You have the power to exercise your will. These facts are true of you because you are a person made in the image of a personal God.

The account of the creation of man in Genesis 1 is a general statement of the fact of creation; the account in Genesis 2 is a more particular account of the method that God used.

> "And the LORD God formed man of the dust of the ground, and breathed into his nostrils the breath of life; and man became a living being" (Genesis 2:7).

From this passage and others it appears that man has a threefold nature: *body*, *spirit*, and *soul*.

Body. The part of man formed from the ground was his body. From science we know that a number of the chemical elements found in the soil (such as carbon, hydrogen, oxygen, and nitrogen) are found also in the human body.

Spirit. God breathed the "breath of life" into Adam. The word which is translated "breath" is sometimes translated "spirit."

Soul. Genesis 2 says that "man became a living soul [being]" (KJV)

In the New Testament we have this verse that delineates these same three parts of man's being.

> "May your whole spirit, soul, and body be preserved blameless at the coming of our Lord Jesus Christ" (1 Thessalonians 5:23).

While it is true that sometimes in Scripture the terms *spirit* and *soul* are used interchangeably, there are other passages, such as those just quoted, in which a distinction is made between the two. When used without distinction, both terms refer to the immaterial components of man in contrast to his body, which is material.

When, however, we make a sharper analysis, the spirit is seen to be that part of man which gives him God-consciousness. This God-consciousness enables him to worship and love God and to have fellowship with Him. Animals do not have this capacity because they were not made in the image and likeness of God.

As a living soul, a self-conscious being, man has power to think and reason, and power to give expression to his emotions. He has intellect, emotions, and will. Adam exercised his power of thought, for instance, when he gave names to all the animals God had created (Genesis 2:19).

God made man innocent, yet having a free will. Man had the choice of obeying or disobeying God (Genesis 2:16-17). The very fact that man was made in the image of God rules out the possibility that man was ever a mere machine or robot.

God created man as a race—"male and female He created them" (Genesis 1:27). Thus, all human beings who ever lived or who ever will live are related to one another (Acts 17:26).

God created man with the intention that man would have dominion over the whole earth and all its creatures.

> *"God blessed them, and God said to them, 'Be fruitful and multiply;increase in number; fill the earth and subdue it; have dominion over the fish of the sea and over the birds of the air and over every living thing that moves on the earth'" (Genesis 1:28).*

Psalm 8 speaks of this dominion that man received from God. The defiling nature of sin has affected how man exerts his authority and stewardship of the earth. In Hebrews 2:5-10, the inspired writer quotes from this psalm to show how it foretold the coming Savior and to teach us that, when He rules in righteousness and peace over the earth, He will exercise all the power over His creation that Adam lost through sin—and more!

> *"For He has not put the world to come, of which we speak, in subjection to angels. But one testified in a certain place, saying: 'What is man that You are mindful of him, Or the son of man that You take care of him? You have made him a little lower than the angels; You have crowned him with glory and honor, And set him over the works of Your hands. You have put all things in subjection under his feet.' For in that He put all in subjection under him, He left nothing that is not put under him. But now we do not yet see all things put under him. But we see Jesus, who was made a little lower than the angels, for the suffering of death crowned with glory and honor, that He, by the grace of God, might taste death for everyone. For it was fitting for Him, for whom are all things and by whom are all things, in bringing many sons to glory, to make the captain of their salvation perfect through sufferings" (Hebrews 2:5-10).*

By the grace of God, redeemed sinners will share in that glorious reign of the King of righteousness and peace.

God's Purpose in Creating Man

What was God's objective in putting man on the earth? Was it only that man might have a good time in his own way and do as he pleased in all things? Was man made for his own sake, or was he made for the sake of someone else? Surely, the very fact that God made man in His own image proves that He wanted man to have fellowship with Him, to relate to Him. He wanted man to love, serve, and obey Him. Speaking of Christ as Creator, Paul said,

> *"For by Him all things were created. . . . All things were created through Him and for Him" (Colossians 1:16)*

The anthem of praise to Christ in heaven is,

> *"You are worthy, O Lord, to receive glory, and honor, and power; for You created all things, and by Your will they exist and were created" (Revelation 4:11).*

Speaking of mature believers who follow the example that Christ set, Peter wrote,

> *"He does not live the rest of his earthly life for evil human desires, but rather for the will of God" (1 Peter 4:2).* See also 2 Corinthians 5:15; 1 Corinthians 6:19, 20; and Galatians 2:20.

Then, again, while God wants us to please Him in all things, He tells us if we seek to do His will, we will find our chief joy in doing that very thing. God knew that we would need enjoyment, and He lovingly gave us the best there was in the universe to enjoy—He gave us Himself!

> *"After this, the word of the L<small>ORD</small> came to Abram in a vision, saying: 'Do not be afraid, Abram. I am your shield, your exceedingly great reward'" (Genesis 15:1).*

> *"'The L<small>ORD</small> is my portion,' says my soul; 'therefore I hope in Him!'" (Lamentations 3:24)*

> *"'Assuredly, I [Jesus] say to you, there is no one who has left house or parents or brothers or wife or children, for the sake of the kingdom of God, who shall not receive many times more in this present time, and in the age to come eternal life'" (Luke 18:29-30).* See also Philippians 3:7-8 and Psalm 16:5.

Man's Moral Test in Eden

> "The LORD God took the man and put him in the garden of Eden to tend and keep it. And the LORD God commanded the man, saying, 'Of every tree of the garden you may freely eat; but of the tree of the knowledge of good and evil you shall not eat; for in the day that you eat of it you shall surely die'" (Genesis 2:15-17).

You see that this was a very simple command, but it was enough to test man's obedience to God. Here, in an uncomplicated way, with man in a lovely environment and with all his needs supplied, a question was to be decided: Would man obey God or not? Would he stay within the bounds God had set or go beyond them? That the issue was so simple makes the disobedience all the more tragic.

The Fall of Man

Our first parents disobeyed God's command. God gave them liberty to choose to obey Him or their own desires, and they chose the latter. They thus fell from their state of innocence by sinning against God. Read about this now in Genesis chapter 3. Verse 6 reads, "When the woman saw that the tree was good for food, and that it was pleasant to the eyes, and a tree desirable to make one wise, she took of its fruit and ate. She also gave to her husband with her, and he ate."

It is interesting to note that, in the New Testament, Paul deals with this account as the description of an actual, historical event (Romans 5:12). A parallel (doctrinal) passage is found in 1 John 2:16, where the world is said to consist of the "the lust of the flesh, the lust of the eyes and the pride of life," the same three elements that were present in the temptation of Eve.

These passages teach us that even the best of us ought not to trust in our own strength to resist Satan. Rather, we must trust in God! Adam was created innocent, and yet he was not strong enough to resist this temptation. How much weaker, therefore, must we be in our sinful nature!

Our first parents made the great mistake of not believing God; they failed to take Him at His word; they failed to trust in Him and His provisions for them; they did not discern that His will had their best interests at heart.

> *"But without faith it is impossible to please Him, for he who comes to God must believe that He is, and that He is a rewarder of those who diligently seek Him" (Hebrews 11:6).*

The Results of the Fall

In our next lesson we will consider sin and its consequences, but first, let's consider one question. God said to Adam and Eve that if they ate of the forbidden fruit, at that moment they would surely die; yet they lived for nearly a thousand years after their sin! (See Genesis 5:1-5.) How are we to explain this?

The word *death* essentially means "separation." In Scripture there are three kinds of death. Physical death is the separation of the soul from the body. Spiritual death is the separation of the individual from God by sin:

> *"And you . . . who were dead in tresspasses and sins . . ." (Ephesians 2:1).*

The spiritual death of Adam and Eve took place the very day they ate of the forbidden fruit; Genesis 3:8 tells us that they tried to hide themselves from the presence of God. At the same time, decay began to enter into their bodies, which later caused their physical death. God put them out of the garden of Eden, a picture of their being separated from Him spiritually due to their sinful state.

Eternal death, or "the second death" (Revelation 20:14-15) will be the fate of all unbelievers in a place the Bible describes as "the lake of fire," a place of punishment for all eternity. But God does not want human beings to go there. He did not make us for that. He made us to enjoy Him, not only in this world, but also in the world to come.

> *"'For I have no pleasure in the death of one who dies,' says the Lord God. 'Therefore turn and live!'" (Ezekiel 18:32).* Compare 2 Peter 3:9.

Just think of it—an eternity of enjoyment is before those who have begun to enjoy God here! Have you begun to enjoy Him?

CHAPTER

6

What the Bible Says About Sin

It has been said that those who have light views of sin will have little appreciation of salvation. If we are ever tempted to minimize the awfulness of sin, we should remember that it was sin which made it necessary for the Son of God to become a man and suffer and die upon the cross.

Some people try to get rid of sin by denying its existence altogether. However, the Bible declares sin to be a terrible reality.

What Is Sin?

In simple terms, sin can be defined as any thought, word, or deed that does not meet God's perfect standard as revealed in His Word and in the incarnation of His Son. There are different synonymns for sin used in the Bible, like iniquity, transgression, lawlessness, disobedience, etc. Each one conveys a different aspect of the word, like missing the mark or overstepping a set boundary line.

> *"For all have sinned and fall short of the glory of God"* (Romans 3:23).

> *"Whoever commits sin also commits lawlessness, and sin is lawlessness"* (1 John 3:4).

It is important for us to understand what is meant by the law of God. Perhaps we think of the law of God as only the Ten Commandments. But if we look at Romans 2:13-15 ("for when Gentiles, who do not have the law, by nature do the things in the law, these, although not having the law, are a law to themselves, who show the work of the law written in their hearts, their conscience also bearing witness, and between themselves their thoughts accusing or else excusing them"), we see that God has written a "law" on the hearts of men (v. 15). We all know what that law is. We all know when we break that law. Every time we do wrong there is something within our conscience that tells us so.

The Universality of Sin

Now that we know what sin is, we are brought face to face with the awful fact that by the fall, our parents brought all mankind into a state of sin and misery. For example, Adam and Eve brought the first human child into the world and named him Cain. He became a murderer! How quickly the Adamic, fallen nature reared its ugly head! This sinful nature has been passed on from generation to generation in human procreation.

Not only are human beings sinners by nature, transmitting sin from generation to generation, but the sin of Adam has been imputed (credited) to every human being:

> *"Therefore, just as through one man sin entered the world, and death through sin, and thus death spread to all men, because all sinned..." (Romans 5:12).* Compare Genesis 3:16-19, 22, 24 with Romans 5:12, 18-19.

Sin and Sins

1. The Sin Nature

Because all of us were in Adam when he sinned, every human being who has been born into the world, with the exception of Jesus Christ, has been born with a sinful nature.

> *"For as by one man's disobedience many were made sinners..." (Romans 5:19).*

This is sometimes spoken of as *original sin* or *total depravity*. Adam, the first of all mankind, sinned and brought the whole race into pain, sorrow, death, and judgment. He was our representative. (Although, technically, Eve sinned first, Adam was the one to whom God gave the commandment, and God did that before Eve was created, Genesis 2:16-17.) Adam stood in our place before God just as, centuries later, Jesus Christ—who is called in

Scripture the "last Adam" (1 Corinthians 15:45)—stood in our place before God. The Lord Jesus regained for us what Adam lost, even as the latter part of Romans 5:19 definitively states: "So also by one Man's obedience many will be made righteous."

As we were born with a sinful nature inherited from Adam, we all "were by nature children of wrath" (Ephesians 2:3). It may be some time after our birth before we begin to give evidence that we are sinners, but we will undoubtedly soon sin and leave no room for argument that we were born sinful. We have all seen that a child does not need to be taught to sin. This is because he has inherited a sin nature from Adam, and so it is in his nature to sin.

The term "total depravity" does not mean that every individual is as bad as he could be, but that the corruption of sin runs through our whole being. The Bible declares that those apart from Christ are "dead in trespasses and sins" (Ephesians 2:1). The sin of Adam is in our souls and spirits, as well as in our bodies.

> "Then the LORD saw that the wickedness of man was great in the earth, and that every intent of the thoughts of his heart was only evil continually" (Genesis 6:5).

This total depravity may also be described as a lack of original righteousness. There is nothing within any of us by nature that could stand the test before our holy and righteous God.

> "As it is written: 'There is none righteous, no not one'" (Romans 3:10).

2. The Fruit of the Sin Nature

From the original sin, which is our nature, come the sins that are manifest in our lives. From the root comes the fruit. We have not become sinners because we sinned; rather, we sin because we are sinners. Sins in our lives may be actual transgressions; they also may be the disobedience of not doing what God commands.

> "For out of the heart proceed evil thoughts, murders, adulteries, fornications, thefts, false witness, blasphemies" (Matthew 15:19).

See also the description of men as sinners in Romans 3:9-20.

The fiendish evil displayed by civilized men in the wars throughout our history shows the folly of the idea that man is gradually improving morally. The Lord Jesus said to Nicodemus: "Unless one is born again, he cannot see the kingdom of God" (John 3:3). Nothing other than being born from above will fit man to live and serve under His authority.

Five Results of Sin

1. Loss of Communion with God

> "And you, who once were enemies and alienated in your mind by wicked works . . ." (Colossians 1:21).

Loss of communion with God means we are separated from Him through sin and disobedience. This is described in Scripture as spiritual death (Ephesians 2:1). As soon as Adam and Eve sinned, their fellowship with God was broken; they could not stand in His holy presence unashamed and unafraid. Neither could the holy God tolerate sin!

> "So He drove out the man out, and He placed cherubim at the east of the garden of Eden, and a flaming sword which turned every way to guard the way to the tree of life" (Genesis 3:24).

Adam and Eve no longer had the same intimate fellowship with God as they had before. They were now separated from Him; all men have been separated from God in spirit ever since. Nor can any of us be brought back into fellowship or communion with Him except through the one Mediator, Jesus Christ.

2. The Condemnation of God

Condemnation implies blame. God holds us accountable for our sin. We are like criminals who have been tried, found guilty, and sentenced to be punished. In this sense, every one of us is already lost until we place our faith in the Lord Jesus Christ.

> "He who believes in Him [Christ] is not condemned; but he who does not believe is condemned already; because he has not believed in the name of the only begotten Son of God" (John 3:18).

> *"He who believes in the Son has everlasting life; and he who does not believe the Son shall not see life, but the wrath of God abides on him" (John 3:36).*

3. Earthly Unhappiness

All the unhappiness in this world is part of the misery of sin. We would never have known sorrow, sadness, and death but for the fall. This does not mean that individual sinners are always unhappy. The psalmist was troubled when he saw the wicked prospering, as is often the case temporarily. He was reminded by the Spirit of God, however, of "their end." (See Psalm 73, especially verse 7.)

4. Death

Death, whether spiritual or physical, is the result of sin. Paul shows in Romans 5:12-21 how Adam's sin caused death to reign; therefore even infants, who have not committed personal sins, die. Physical death is the separation of the soul and spirit from the body. It is an enemy that will be finally destroyed at the end of Christ's millennial reign. "Then death and Hades were cast into the lake of fire. This is the second death" (Revelation 20:14).

> *"For the wages of sin is death, but the gift of God is eternal life in Christ Jesus our Lord" (Romans 6:23).*

5. Eternal Punishment

Eternal punishment is a solemn fact of Scripture that cannot be ignored. If God is eternal, and if the condition of the saved is eternal, then the punishment of the lost must be eternal, for the same word is used in reference to them all.

> *"These [the people who do not obey the gospel of our Lord Jesus Christ, see v. 8] shall be punished with everlasting destruction from the presence of the Lord and from the glory of His power" (2 Thessalonians 1:9).*

The Lord Jesus Christ said more about hell than did anyone else in Scripture. He wants us to see the awful danger we are in and to flee to Him for refuge. Those who will not accept Him as Savior will have Him as Judge.

> *"Then He [Christ the King] will also say to those on the left hand, 'Depart from Me, you cursed, into the everlasting fire prepared for the devil and his angels'" (Matthew 25:41).*

God's Remedy for Man's Sin Problem

This teaching about sin forms a black backdrop against which the jewel of God's grace shines even more brightly. As the prophet Jonah declared, "Salvation is of the LORD" (Jonah 2:9). God manifested His love and grace by giving His Son, the Lord Jesus Christ, to save us from eternal judgment. Christ is the only One who can deliver men and women, boys and girls, out of sin and misery and bring us into a state of salvation.

> *"But when the kindness and love of God our Savior appeared, not by works of righteousness which we have done, but according to His mercy He saved us, through the washing of regeneration and renewal of the Holy Spirit, whom He poured out on us abundantly through Jesus Christ our Savior" (Titus 3:4-6).*

The ground of our salvation is the redemptive work of Christ, which will be discussed in a later lesson. The source of our salvation is God's grace. The channel through which it is received is faith. God does not save us because we deserve it, or because we can demand His mercy, but simply because it is His good pleasure to do so.

> *"For by grace you have been saved through faith, and that not of yourselves; it is the gift of God, not of works, lest anyone should boast" (Ephesians 2:8-9).*

Grace is unmerited, undeserved favor. The saved sinner receives the very opposite of what he deserves. "For God so loved the world that He gave His only begotten Son, that whoever believes in Him should not perish but have everlasting life" (John 3:16).

THE BIBLE SPEAKS

Exam Booklet
AK '15 (1 Unit) TBS

STUDENT NAME (PLEASE PRINT)

ADDRESS

CITY, STATE, ZIP

COURSE GRADE: _____

INSTRUCTOR

Exam developed by Emmaus Correspondence School, founded in 1942.

A NOTE ON THE EXAMS

The exams are designed to check your knowledge of the course material and the Scriptures. After you have studied a chapter, review the exam questions for that lesson. If you have difficulty in answering the questions, re-read the material. If questions contain a Scripture reference, you may use your Bible to help you answer them. If your instructor has provided a Single Page Answer Sheet, record your answer on that sheet. This exam contains the following types of questions:

TRUE / FALSE

For these questions, circle the correct answer.　　　　　　　　(T)　F

MULTIPLE CHOICE

You will be asked to write in the letter of the correct answer at the space on the right. Here is an example:

The color of grass is
- A. blue
- B. green
- C. yellow　　　　　　　　　　　　　　　　　　　　　　　**B**

WHAT DO YOU SAY?

Under this heading we invite you to put into words something you have learned from that chapter, and to share that with us.

RETURNING THE EXAM

See the back of this exam booklet for instructions on returning your exam for grading.

⟨ **DO NOT PHOTOCOPY THESE EXAM PAGES** ⟩

First Edition 2015 (AK '15), 1 UNIT

ISBN 978-1-59387-228-1

Code: TBS

Copyright © 2015 ECS Ministries

All rights reserved. No part of this publication may be reproduced or transmitted in any form or by any means, electronic or mechanical.

Printed in the United States of America

CHAPTER 1 EXAM

What the Bible Says About the Bible

EXAM GRADE _____

Before starting this exam, write your name and address on the front of this Exam Booklet.

Read each statement carefully and circle the letter of the correct answer: T—if true, or F—if false. Use the separate answer sheet if provided.

1. The Bible was written by verbal inspiration, God giving the actual words of the original Scriptures. T F

2. Because the Bible is true, we can have complete confidence in what it says. T F

3. The Bible reveals a few of the ways by which we can experience salvation. T F

4. Fortune telling is mentioned favorably in the Bible. T F

5. In the Bible, God has told us about Himself and our relationship with Him. T F

Write the letter of the correct answer in the blank space on the right. Use the separate answer sheet if provided.

6. The doctrine of plenary inspiration teaches that
   A. only parts of the Bible are inspired.
   B. the human writers of the Bible all wrote in the same style.
   C. all parts of the Bible are equally authoritative. _____

7. We can discover the truth about God and His relationship to the world
   A. only as He reveals it to us.
   B. by ordinary human means.
   C. in the traditions of the church. _____

8. The expression *the Word* applies to
   A. the Scriptures only.
   B. Christ only.
   C. Christ and the Scriptures. _____

9. The only way to be made right with God is to
   A. attend church regularly.
   B. believe in the gospel of Jesus Christ.
   C. complete good works.

10. In the book of _____ we learn much about the future.
    A. Revelation
    B. Philemon
    C. Genesis

What Do You Say?

Write here one thing you have learned from this lesson.

_____
_____
_____
_____

CHAPTER 2 EXAM

What the Bible Says About God

EXAM GRADE

Circle the letter of the correct answer: T—if true, or F—if false.
Use the separate answer sheet if provided.

1. The writers of the Bible tried to prove the existence of God.   T   F

2. God is an impersonal force.   T   F

3. The terms *justice* and *righteousness* are used interchangeably in the Scriptures.   T   F

4. Because God is absolute Truth, we can rely on Him to fulfill His promises.   T   F

5. Romans 5:8 tells us how God showed His love for us.   T   F

Write the letter of the correct answer in the blank space on the right.
Use the separate answer sheet if provided.

6. God is unchangeable; this means that He
   A. is perfect, and perfection knows no change.
   B. has always existed.
   C. changes His personality to fit our needs.   _____

7. God's natural attributes are
   A. qualities of His being that apply to us too.
   B. qualities of His being that He alone can claim.
   C. qualities such as wisdom, truth, and love, which He can give to anybody He chooses.   _____

8. The term *omnipresence*, applied to God, means that
   A. He has been present in this world since it was created.
   B. God is a rare material substance that covers the universe.
   C. God is an infinite Spirit who is personally present everywhere.   _____

9. In the world there are many gods. What does the Bible say about these gods?
   A. They are worthless.
   B. They represent other ways of salvation.
   C. They are just other names for the true God of the Bible. _____

10. God offers us
    A. an easy life with no problems.
    B. eternal life with Him.
    C. nothing in this world. _____

WHAT DO YOU SAY?

Write here one thing you have learned from this lesson.

_____

_____

_____

_____

THE BIBLE SPEAKS　　　　　　　　　　　　　　　　　　　　　　　　AK '15

CHAPTER 3 EXAM

What the Bible Says About the Trinity

EXAM GRADE _____

Circle the letter of the correct answer: T—if true, or F—if false.
Use the separate answer sheet if provided.

1. In the Bible, each person in the Trinity is referred to at different times as God.　　　　T　F

2. The concept of the three persons of the Trinity, according to the lesson material, is one of multiplication rather than addition.　　　　T　F

3. The doctrine of the Trinity is understandable by everyone.　　　　T　F

4. Christians are to be baptized in the names of the Father, the Son, and the Holy Spirit.　　　　T　F

5. The members of the Trinity are one in being, essence, power.　　　　T　F

Write the letter of the correct answer in the blank space on the right.
Use the separate answer sheet if provided.

6. In the Old Testament, there are indications that
    A. God exists in only one person, the Father.
    B. God is one of many beings who rule the universe.
    C. God exists in a plurality of persons.　　　　_____

7. In John's gospel, John references a quotation from the prophet _____ that supports Christ's deity.
    A. Jeremiah
    B. Isaiah
    C. Daniel　　　　_____

8. Which statement is true concerning the relative positions of the three persons of the Trinity?
   A. God the Father is superior to God the Son and God the Holy Spirit.
   B. Because He partook of human nature, God the Son is inferior to the other two persons of the Trinity.
   C. God the Father, God the Son, and God the Holy Spirit are equally and absolutely God.

9. At what important event in the life of Jesus was the Trinity manifested?
   A. The birth of Jesus
   B. The baptism of Jesus
   C. The crucifixion

10. If we categorize the different activities of the members of the Godhead, we can see that the Holy Spirit's work involves
    A. initiating and operating.
    B. creating and redeeming.
    C. ministering and producing.

What Do You Say?

Write here one thing you have learned from this lesson.

_____
_____
_____
_____

CHAPTER 4 EXAM

WHAT THE BIBLE SAYS ABOUT GOD'S RELATION TO THE WORLD

EXAM GRADE

Circle the letter of the correct answer: T—if true, or F—if false.
Use the separate answer sheet if provided.

1. The evolutionist can easily explain the origin of the first matter in the universe.   T   F

2. In the New Testament, Christ is spoken of as the Creator of all things.   T   F

3. All the evil in this world is the result of sin.   T   F

4. It is more reasonable to believe that this complicated world has a sovereign Ruler than that it is carried along by blind chance.   T   F

5. God will someday create new heavens and a new earth.   T   F

Write the letter of the correct answer in the blank space on the right.
Use the separate answer sheet if provided.

6. The question of the origin of the universe is one that has puzzled thinking people for a very long time. Which verse settles the question as far as the Christian is concerned?
   A. Genesis 1:1
   B. Romans 9:20-21
   C. Colossians 1:17

7. God, through Jesus Christ, has made the world
   A. and allows it to take care of itself.
   B. has put the angels in charge of caring for the earth.
   C. and Christ Himself sustains it with His power.

8. Since God has made us, He
   A. let's us do what we think is best for ourselves.
   B. set the rules by which we should live.
   C. sets *righteous* governments in place to rule us.

9. According to Romans 8:21-22, in the future God will deliver the world from the bondage that currently causes it to groan and labor. This bondage came about because of
   A. the danger of going to hell.
   B. money and the love of it.
   C. sin and the corruption of man's nature.

10. We can learn about God's plan for the world
    A. in the Bible.
    B. through studying philosophy.
    C. by comparing the teachings of the major world religions.

What Do You Say?

Write here one thing you have learned from this lesson.

_____
_____
_____
_____

CHAPTER 5 EXAM

What the Bible Says About the Creation and Fall of Man

EXAM GRADE _____

Circle the letter of the correct answer: T—if true, or F—if false. Use the separate answer sheet if provided.

1. Adam was an intelligent human being, capable of naming the animals God had created. T F

2. Man had to undergo a series of complicated tests before God knew that he was disobedient. T F

3. To resist "the lust of the flesh, the lust of the eyes, and the pride of life," God expects Christians to trust in our own strength. T F

4. Man's chief purpose in life should be to enjoy himself and have a good time. T F

5. There are three kinds of death—spiritual death, physical death, and intellectual death. T F

Write the letter of the correct answer in the blank space on the right. Use the separate answer sheet if provided.

6. The biblical record of the creation of man
   A. shows that God formed man from the earth.
   B. displays the power of the angels.
   C. proves evolution. _____

7. The spiritual part of man enables him to
   A. write music.
   B. learn mathematics.
   C. worship God. _____

8. God put man on the earth for the purpose of
   A. enjoying life to the fullest.
   B. caring for the animals.
   C. loving and serving Him. _____

9. The biblical record of the fall of man
   A. is only symbolic of the conflict between good and evil.
   B. reveals that our first parents did not take God at His word.
   C. concludes with the immediate physical death of Adam and Eve.

10. When Adam and Eve sinned,
    A. they retained their spiritual life.
    B. they died spiritually.
    C. they looked forward to meeting God with joyful anticipation.

What Do You Say?

Write here one thing you have learned from this lesson.

_____

_____

_____

_____

CHAPTER 6 EXAM

WHAT THE BIBLE SAYS ABOUT SIN

EXAM GRADE

Circle the letter of the correct answer: T—if true, or F—if false.
Use the separate answer sheet if provided.

1. The law of God is simply another name for the Ten Commandments.   T   F

2. Adam's sin brought sin to the whole human race.   T   F

3. We are sinners because we sin.   T   F

4. Jesus Christ saves us all from eternal judgment.   T   F

5. There are no significant results or ramifications of sin.   T   F

Write the letter of the correct answer in the blank space on the right.
Use the separate answer sheet if provided.

6. Romans 3:23 conveys to us that
    A. sin is all right in certain situations.
    B. all have sinned and come short of God's glory.
    C. sin needs to be erased through good works.   _____

7. A baby
    A. is a sinner from birth.
    B. has to be taught to sin.
    C. learns to sin from observing other people sin.   _____

8. The term *total depravity* means
    A. we are all as evil as we can be.
    B. the corruption of sin runs through our whole being.
    C. our bodies can do evil, but our spirits are pure.   _____

9. In Scripture, hell is mentioned most frequently by
    A. Paul.
    B. Peter.
    C. Christ.   _____

10. The Lord Jesus Christ, in His sacrifice on the cross,
    A. saves those who believe in Him from eternal judgment.
    B. gives to those who believe in Him everlasting life.
    C. Both A and B.

What Do You Say?

Write here one thing you have learned from this lesson.

_____
_____
_____
_____

CHAPTER 7 EXAM

WHAT THE BIBLE SAYS
ABOUT THE PERSON OF CHRIST

EXAM GRADE

Circle the letter of the correct answer: T—if true, or F—if false.
Use the separate answer sheet if provided.

1. The Bible teaches that Christ is eternal, unchangeable, omnipotent, and omniscient. T F

2. Jesus possessed only a human nature. T F

3. As the Son of God, Jesus faced none of the normal problems of life. T F

4. The miracles of Jesus are questionable and should be separated from His teachings. T F

5. One evidence of Jesus' actual resurrection is the fact that the grave clothes were left in the tomb. T F

Write the letter of the correct answer in the blank space on the right.
Use the separate answer sheet if provided.

6. When Christ became a man, He
   A. ceased to be God.
   B. possessed absolute deity and true humanity.
   C. only took on the appearance of humanity without actually becoming a man. _____

7. Christ's humanity is shown by
   A. His being tired and thirsty.
   B. His being born in Jerusalem.
   C. the love and care shown for Him by His brothers. _____

8. Christ's death on the cross was acceptable to God to atone for sin because
   A. He is a finite being like man.
   B. He suffered so much at the hands of men.
   C. He was sinless. _____

9. To provide man with eternal salvation, God had to take on human flesh because
   A. God cannot die.
   B. none of the angels were good enough.
   C. He had failed to get man's attention any other way. _____

10. The resurrected Christ was seen at one time by
    A. all the Jewish leaders who had put Him to death.
    B. about 500 believers.
    C. Pilate and his wife. _____

What Do You Say?

Write here one thing you have learned from this lesson.

_____
_____
_____
_____

THE BIBLE SPEAKS   AK '15

CHAPTER 8 EXAM

WHAT THE BIBLE SAYS
ABOUT THE WORK OF CHRIST

EXAM GRADE _____

Circle the letter of the correct answer: T—if true, or F—if false.
Use the separate answer sheet if provided.

1. By His death, the Lord Jesus satisfied divine justice and made up for the dishonor that the sin of man brought on God's name.   T   F

2. Jesus fully expected that the nation of Israel would accept Him as its King.   T   F

3. The Bible refers to Christ as the "King of the church."   T   F

4. Someday Christ will rule as King over all the earth.   T   F

5. Jesus Christ fulfills the threefold office of Prophet, Priest, and King.   T   F

Write the letter of the correct answer in the blank space on the right.
Use the separate answer sheet if provided.

6. The reason animal sacrifices were offered in the Old Testament was
   A. to provide food for the priests.
   B. to point forward to the Lord Jesus Christ as the Sacrifice for sin.
   C. to take away the guilt and penalty of the Israelites' sin.   _____

7. In the doctrine of reconciliation,
   A. we must receive Christ to experience it.
   B. everyone has been automatically forgiven.
   C. we must work to retain it.   _____

8. The Lord Jesus is presented as our Great High Priest in the book of
   A. John.
   B. Leviticus.
   C. Hebrews.   _____

EXAM BOOKLET

9. In reference to the church, the Bible calls Christ
   A. the Head of the church.
   B. the Servant of the church.
   C. the Guide of the church.

10. When we look to the future, we are told in the Bible that
    A. all things will continue as they are now.
    B. Christ will return to set up His kingdom.
    C. the nations will rise up and establish their kingdom.

WHAT DO YOU SAY?

Write here one thing you have learned from this lesson.

_____

_____

_____

_____

CHAPTER 9 EXAM

What the Bible Says About the Holy Spirit

EXAM GRADE _____

Circle the letter of the correct answer: T—if true, or F—if false.
Use the separate answer sheet if provided.

1. The Holy Spirit is one of the three persons of the Godhead.   T   F
2. The Holy Spirit makes our sin and our need of a Savior real to us.   T   F
3. We receive the baptism of the Spirit at the moment we are born again.   T   F
4. Nothing can hinder the Holy Spirit from filling believers.   T   F
5. The human body is described in the Bible as the Holy Spirit's palace.   T   F

Write the letter of the correct answer in the blank space on the right.
Use the separate answer sheet if provided.

6. The personality of the Holy Spirit is clearly shown by
   A. the use of the neuter pronoun, "it."
   B. the use of the masculine pronoun, "he."
   C. the use of the word "influence."   _____

7. The Holy Spirit _____ the world of sin.
   A. cleanses
   B. convicts
   C. censures   _____

8. The special ministry of the Holy Spirit in connection with those who put their faith in Christ to be saved is
   A. regeneration.
   B. creation.
   C. revelation.   _____

9. Being filled with the Holy Spirit is only for
   A. believers in Christ.
   B. Christian leaders and preachers.
   C. angels.   _____

10. The Holy Spirit is the Christian's
    A. Teacher.
    B. Comforter.
    C. both A & B.   _____

WHAT DO YOU SAY?

Write here one thing you have learned from this lesson.

_____
_____
_____
_____

CHAPTER 10 EXAM

WHAT THE BIBLE SAYS ABOUT FAITH AND REPENTANCE

EXAM GRADE _____

Circle the letter of the correct answer: T—if true, or F—if false. Use the separate answer sheet if provided.

1. Faith and repentance cannot be separated.   T   F

2. Those who trust partly in Christ and partly in their own good works show true faith in Christ.   T   F

3. The word repentance means "a change of mind" away from sin and toward God.   T   F

4. A genuine Christian will be sorry for any sins he commits and will confess them to God.   T   F

5. God is willing to save everyone.   T   F

Write the letter of the correct answer in the blank space on the right. Use the separate answer sheet if provided.

6. Habbakuk 2:4 says, "The just shall live by _____"
   - A. his works
   - B. his prayers
   - C. his faith   _____

7. When a person exercises faith in Christ for salvation,
   - A. he is worried about eternal judgment.
   - B. he has peace with God.
   - C. he still trusts in his own good works.   _____

8. Repentance means
   - A. feeling sorry about one's sin.
   - B. changing one's mind regarding sin.
   - C. taking charge of one's life.   _____

9. Which of these verses refer specifically to salvation?
   - A. Matthew 3:17
   - B. Luke 12:34
   - C. Acts 3:19   _____

10. The only thing necessary to salvation is
    A. doing good works and thus pleasing God.
    B. faith in the finished work of the Lord Jesus Christ.
    C. faithfully attending church and helping the poor. _____

What Do You Say?

Write here one thing you have learned from this lesson.

_____
_____
_____
_____

CHAPTER 11 EXAM

What the Bible Says About the Christian's Heritage

EXAM GRADE _____

Circle the letter of the correct answer: T—if true, or F—if false. Use the separate answer sheet if provided.

1. Believers are justified by keeping the Law of Moses. T F

2. We are children of God by the new birth and sons of God by adoption. T F

3. All believers have been sanctified in their position or standing before God. T F

4. One of the keys to living a sanctified life as a believer is to yield one's body to God as a living sacrifice. T F

5. A Christian's assurance of salvation is based on believing God's promises about it, his growing likeness to Christ, and the inner witness of the Holy Spirit. T F

Write the letter of the correct answer in the blank space on the right. Use the separate answer sheet if provided.

6. In the Bible, *justification*
   A. is my responsibility to explain my sins.
   B. is a judicious act of God whereby He declares the sinner righteous.
   C. is an ongoing process of confessing sins to God. _____

7. In the Bible, *adoption*
   A. is the same as the new birth.
   B. has to do with our standing as adult sons.
   C. makes us children of God. _____

8. The ultimate sanctification of the believer will take place
   A. soon after his conversion if he tries hard enough to be perfect.
   B. in the future, at the return of Christ.
   C. right now, in complete yieldedness to Christ. _____

9. When a Christian dies,
   A. his spirit dies too.
   B. his spirit remains in the grave with his body.
   C. his spirit will be in Christ's presence.

10. The best thing about heaven will be
    A. seeing Christ face to face.
    B. getting new, glorified bodies.
    C. being reunited with our loved ones.

What Do You Say?

Write here one thing you have learned from this lesson.

_____
_____
_____
_____

THE BIBLE SPEAKS   AK '15

CHAPTER 12 EXAM

WHAT THE BIBLE SAYS ABOUT
LIVING THE CHRISTIAN LIFE

EXAM GRADE

Circle the letter of the correct answer: T—if true, or F—if false.
Use the separate answer sheet if provided.

1. We can expect God to give spiritual knowledge to us without our studying the Bible.   T   F

2. If we are unable to understand something in the Bible, we should refuse to believe it until we do understand it.   T   F

3. We should not trouble God with material or physical needs.   T   F

4. Praying in Jesus' name means to ask on His authority for things He would approve of.   T   F

5. Meeting with other believers regularly is not important to the believer in Christ.   T   F

Write the letter of the correct answer in the blank space on the right.
Use the separate answer sheet if provided.

6. Bible study is important, and 2 Timothy 2:15 exhorts us to be _____ in how we do it.
   A. diligent
   B. quick
   C. serious   _____

7. When we pray, we should remember to
   A. make some kind of promise to God.
   B. always ask for something.
   C. express our thanks to God.   _____

8. Baptism is an outward sign
   A. of our inward spiritual salvation in Christ.
   B. of our formal church membership.
   C. of the need to be cleansed of our sin.   _____

EXAM BOOKLET

9. When we participate in the Lord's Supper, we are demonstrating that
   A. we are one with Christ only.
   B. we are one with each other only.
   C. we are one with Christ and with each other. _____

10. In 2 Timothy 4:7-8, what Paul looks forward to receiving for having "fought the good fight" is
    A. being welcomed into heaven.
    B. the crown of righteousness.
    C. a position of power. _____

What Do You Say?

Write here one thing you have learned from this lesson.

_____
_____
_____
_____

RETURNING THE EXAM BOOKLET FOR GRADING

- ✓ After completing the exam, check it carefully.
- ✓ Make sure you have followed the directions.
- ✓ Be sure you have written your correct name and address on all material you will send to the School.
- ✓ Return all the exams at one time instead of separating and mailing each individual exam.
- ✓ Make sure to very carefully pull the exam booklet out of the middle of the book (you may need to lift up the staples in order to remove it). Return only this exam booklet, not the course book. If you have used the Single Page Answer Sheet, return only that sheet.
- ✓ Address the envelope correctly.
- ✓ Put the correct postage on the envelope.
- ✓ If you are studying this course through an Associate Instructor or associated ministry or organization, send the exams to the individual or organization from which you obtained the course. Otherwise, send them to the address below.

Please return to
Emmaus Bible School UK
Carlett Boulevard
Eastham, Wirral
Merseyside. CH62 8BZ
Tel: 0151 378 7289
www.emmausuk.com

CHAPTER

7

WHAT THE BIBLE SAYS ABOUT THE PERSON OF CHRIST

After the enemies of the Lord Jesus Christ had asked Him questions in which they tried to trap Him, Jesus responded by asking a searching question of them: "What do you think about the Christ? Whose Son is He?" (Matthew 22:42).

This is the most important question you, too, will ever face; your eternal destiny depends on how you answer it. The teaching concerning the person and work of Jesus Christ is the central teaching of the Word of God. We need to be absolutely clear about what the Bible says concerning Him.

Jesus Christ Is God

The Bible teaches that Jesus Christ is God—in the full and absolute sense of the word—and that He is one of the persons of the Holy Trinity. This teaching is called *the deity of Jesus Christ*. Scripture provides many proofs of the deity of Christ, some of which we will study here:

1. He Is Called God

Besides the divine names that are given to Christ, such as Immanuel, which means "God with us" (Isaiah 7:14; Matthew 1:23), there are definite statements in the Scripture that Jesus Christ is God.

"In the beginning was the Word, and the Word was with God, and the Word was God" (John 1:1). This verse shows that the Son of God is as eternal as the Father, with His own personality, and is God just as the Father is God.

> "But about the Son He [God] says, 'Your throne, O God, is forever and ever; a scepter of righteousness is the scepter of Your kingdom'" (Hebrews 1:8).
>
> ". . . And we are in Him who is true, in His Son Jesus Christ. This is the true God and eternal life" (1 John 5:20). See also Romans 9:5; Colossians 1:15; and Hebrews 1:2-3.

2. He Has the Attributes of God

The Bible describes Christ as eternal and unchangeable:

> "In the beginning was the Word" (John 1:1).
>
> "Jesus Christ is the same yesterday, today, and forever" (Hebrews 13:8).
>
> "But You [the Son] are the same, and Your years will not fail" (Hebrews 1:12).

Furthermore, the attributes of God that cannot belong to any creature are said to belong to Christ, like omnipotence (Matthew 28:18; Hebrews 1:3) and omniscience (John 1:48; 2:24-25; 21:17).

3. He Was Active in Creation

We have seen in a previous lesson that God is the Creator. Scripture teaches in many places that Jesus Christ, the Son of God, is the Creator.

> "All things were made through Him, and without Him nothing was made that was made" (John 1:3). See also Colossians 1:16 and Hebrews 1:2.

When He was here on earth He created enough food out of five loaves and two fish to feed more than 5,000 people! See John chapter 6.

4. He Forgives Sins

In Mark chapter 2, when the Lord Jesus told the paralysed man that his sins were forgiven, the scribes condemned Him inwardly, saying, "Who can forgive sins but God alone?" (Mark 2:7).

They were correct in this respect, but wrong in not believing that Jesus is God, for He went on to prove His right to forgive sins by demonstrating His power to heal the sick man.

"But that you may know that the Son of Man has power on earth to forgive sins"—He said to the paralytic, 'I say to you, arise, take up your bed, and go to your house.' Immediately he arose, took up the bed, and went out in the presence of them all" (Mark 2:10-12).

5. He Claimed to Be God

If you believe that Jesus is good and therefore spoke only truth about Himself, the logical conclusion you must reach is that He is God. His enemies understood that He was claiming deity and accused Him of blasphemy. He said:

"I and the Father are one" (John 10:30).

"Anyone who has seen Me has seen the Father" (John 14:9).

Jesus Christ Is the God-Man

There is an old fable about a man who tried to persuade some birds to come into his home out of the intense cold. Although the birds were freezing to death, they refused to come, because they were afraid of him. As the man sought a way to save the birds, he began to realize that he could save their lives only by becoming a bird and communicating with them in their own language. Since he was unable to do this, the birds perished.

"The Word became flesh and dwelt among us" (John 1:14).

This verse tells us that the Lord Jesus Christ is one person with two natures. He is the God-man, possessing absolute deity and true humanity. His becoming man is known as *the Incarnation.*

1. His Birth

The Son of God, a Spirit Being, humbled Himself by being born a human being.

"Who [Jesus], being in the form of God, did not consider it robbery to be equal with God, but made Himself of no reputation, taking the form of a bondservant, and coming in the likeness of men" (Philippians 2:6-7).

He always was the Lord of glory; by Him the worlds were made; and yet He consented to take on human nature (Hebrews 2:14).

He was virgin-born, as Luke 1:34-35 clearly shows. In answer to Mary's question, the angel said, "The Holy Spirit will come upon you, and the power of the Highest will overshadow you; therefore, also, the Holy One who is to be born will be called the Son of God."

His mother was not a queen, just a poor young woman of Nazareth. His birthplace was not a palace, but a stable (Luke 2:7). He had to work for a living as a carpenter (Mark 6:3). He had no permanent home (Matthew 8:20). He lived poor and died poor; He was dependent on the material support of others during His public ministry (Luke 8:1-3).

> *"For you know the grace of our Lord Jesus Christ, that though He was rich, yet for your sakes He became poor, that you through His poverty might become rich"* (2 Corinthians 8:9).

2. His Life

As well as His modest lifestyle, He also experienced human deprivations like fatigue and thirst, and He knew the misery of being misunderstood by relatives and friends: "For even His brothers did not believe in Him" (John 7:5).

> *"For we do not have a High priest who cannot sympathize with our weaknesses, but was in all points tempted as we are, yet without sin"* (Hebrews 4:15).

The ministry of Jesus was marked by teachings and miracles. All attempts to explain His miracles without acknowledging that Jesus possessed supernatural powers are unconvincing. The miracles are woven into the accounts of His life so closely that to deny them is to make the rest of the story meaningless. The miracles show us Jesus Christ truly came from God and is the Son of God.

3. His Death

The fact that Jesus Christ was perfectly holy and sinless meant He could be a perfect sacrifice for sin that was completely acceptable to God. Therefore God poured out His condemnation of sin upon Christ when He was hanging on the cross. The Scripture teaches that our sin was imputed to Him—that is, it was put to His account as though it were His own; it was laid upon Him and counted against Him.

> "God made Him who knew no sin to be sin for us, so that we might become the righteousness of God in Him" (2 Cointhians. 5:21).

> "[He] Himself bore our sins in His own body on the tree, that we, having died to sins, might live for righteousness—by whose stripes you were healed" (1 Peter 2:24). See also Isaiah 53:3-6.

What a terrible humiliation this was for a sinless soul to endure! The fact that He was the Sin-bearer caused the Father, as divine Judge, to forsake Him.

> "About the ninth hour Jesus cried out in a loud voice . . . 'My God, My God, why have You forsaken Me?'" (Matthew 27:46).

Just what our Lord's forsaken cry on the cross means, no human being can possibly know. We only know that it was part of the penalty of sin that He endured for us. It must have been the hardest part, harder than any of the insults He received from men, harder than the pains of crucifixion itself. But we may praise the Father for the blessed fact that He forsook His own Son for a time in order that He might not forsake us forever.

Deity could not die. But because the Son took on human flesh, He *could* die. And because He is God as well as man, the eternal death He endured in three hours of separation from God was the death of an infinite person, thus sufficient to atone for the sins of all who have ever lived (though only effectual for those who appropriate the salvation He purchased for them). No man took His life from Him; when He had paid sin's debt, He dismissed His spirit and died physically (John 10:18; 19:30).

In contrast to some modern theories, the writers of the Gospels clearly state that Jesus really did die. Not only was a spear thrust into His side, but it was the Roman soldiers—well-acquainted with death by crucifixion—who bore witness to His death (John 19:33-34).

4. His Resurrection

The Bible shows us that the humiliation of the Lord Jesus Christ led to His exaltation by God the Father. He accomplished what He came into the world to do and was raised out from among the dead in victory over sin, death, and the devil.

The empty tomb and Jesus' later appearances give evidence of His resurrection. John, coming to the tomb, realized that Christ's body had not been stolen, because the burial clothes were lying there (having been wound around the body of Jesus). No one stealing a body would have left the grave clothes there (John 20:6-8).

As to His post-resurrection appearances, on one occasion more than five hundred persons saw Him. It is highly unlikely that all these people were mistaken about whom they saw:

> *"After that He was seen by over five hundred brethren at once, of whom the greater part remain to the present, but some have fallen asleep"* (1 Corinthians 15:6).

CHAPTER

8

WHAT THE BIBLE SAYS ABOUT THE WORK OF CHRIST

One goal of the work of Christ is to bring men safely through death to spend eternity with Him. The benefits of Christ's work are available to all who will receive Him through putting their faith in Him. In accomplishing the work of redemption, the Lord Jesus Christ fulfills the threefold office of Prophet, Priest, and King.

Christ as Prophet

In the Bible a prophet was one who spoke for God to men—they were His messengers, His mouthpieces. The content of a prophet's message was usually either proclamation ("Thus says the Lord . . .") which took the form of rebuke or encouragement, or of foretelling future events to either warn or comfort his audience. The Lord Jesus was a Prophet in that He proclaimed God's righteous standards for His coming kingdom; He offered Himself as the only source of eternal life and salvation from sin; and He predicted not only His own death and resurrection but many future events as they related to the nation of Israel.

1. Teaching

Time and again we read in the gospel accounts that the Lord Jesus taught the people. The general reaction was amazement. After concluding what is commonly known as the Sermon on the Mount, we read, "And so it was, when Jesus had ended these sayings, that the people were astonished at His teaching, for He taught them as one having authority, and not as the scribes" (Matthew 7:28-29).

2. Proclaiming Himself as Savior

Many of Christ's own words testify to His planned purpose for coming to earth. Here are just four (note, Jesus often referred to Himself as the Son of Man):

> *"For even the Son of Man did not come to served, but to serve, and to give His life a ransom for many" (Mark 10:45).*

> *"For the Son of Man has come to seek and to save that which was lost" (Luke 19:10).*

> *"I have come that they may have life, and that they may have it more abundantly" (John 10:10).*

> *"I am the way, the truth, and the life. No one comes to the Father except through Me" (John 14:6).*

3. Predicting the Future

Here is one of the many occasions when Jesus warned His disciples of what was going to happen to Him:

> *"And He began to teach them that the Son of Man must suffer many things, and be rejected by the elders and chief priests and scribes, and be killed, and after three days rise again" (Mark 8:31).*

Mark 13 is a whole chapter in which Jesus described conditions when Jerusalem would be destroyed (which happened in AD 70) and in the seven-year tribulation period that is still future. His warning was,

> *"Take heed, watch and pray; for you do not know when the time is" (Mark 13:33).*

Christ as Priest

A priest is one who represents men before God, who offers sacrifices on behalf of the people, and who intercedes as a go-between or mediator between God and man.

The Lord Jesus Christ is presented in the Bible as a Priest, especially in the epistle to the Hebrews (e.g. Hebrews 4:14, and chapters 7-10).

1. Christ as Our Priest Offered a Sacrifice

The animal sacrifices of the Old Testament, while ordained by God to be used temporarily as atonement or covering for sin, could not take away the guilt and penalty of sin. They all pointed forward to the Lord Jesus Christ who offered Himself as our sacrifice, one that was complete and once-for-all.

John the Baptist, seeing Jesus, said, "Behold! the Lamb of God who takes away the sin of the world!" (John 1:29).

Jesus' death as the Lamb of God was a substitutionary sacrifice. During the war in Vietnam, an enemy hand grenade was thrown into the midst of a small group of American soldiers. One soldier threw himself on the grenade and was instantly killed as it exploded. He chose to die that his friends might live. This is but a faint illustration of the substitutionary death of the Lord Jesus Christ.

Christ was both the Offerer and the Offering, both the Priest and the Sacrifice. In giving Himself to die for us upon the cross, He accomplished the work for which He came. This atoning work is often referred to as "the finished work of Christ." It includes three major elements.

a. Propitiation

Propitiation means this: By His death, the Lord Jesus Christ satisfied divine justice and made up for the dishonor which the sin of man had brought on God's name and authority. Holy God could only forgive sinners on righteous grounds, for He cannot compromise with sin. That righteous ground—the death of God's Son—had been in the plan of the Godhead in eternity past (1 Peter 1:20).

> "God set [Jesus Christ] forth as a propitiation by His blood, through faith, to demonstrate His righteousness, because in His forbearance God passed over the sins that were previously committed, to demonstrate at the present time His righteousness, that He might be just and the justifier of the one who has faith in Jesus" (Romans 3:25-26).

> "He Himself is the propitiation for our sins . . ." (1 John 2:2).

b. Redemption

The Bible teaches that sin placed us under a terrible bondage from which the Lord Jesus, by His death, delivers us.

> *"For all have sinned and fall short of the glory of God, being justified freely by His grace through the redemption that is in Christ Jesus" (Romans 3:23-24).* See also Ephesians 1:7 and Colossians 1:14.

The purchase price of our redemption was the sacrificial death of Christ.

> *"For you know that it was not with perishable things such as silver or gold that you were redeemed from the empty way of life handed down to you from your forefathers, but with the precious blood of Christ, a lamb without blemish or defect" (1 Peter 1:18-19).*

> *". . . Without the shedding of blood there is no remission [forgiveness]" (Hebrews 9:22).*

c. Reconciliation

By His death the Lord Jesus Christ provided reconciliation to God. We who were estranged from God could now be restored to fellowship with Him. This reconciliation has been made potentially for all; however, the reconciliation does not become a reality in one's life until he or she receives Christ.

> *"But now in Christ Jesus you who once were far off have been brought near by the blood of Christ. For He Himself is our peace, who has made both [Jews and Gentiles] one . . . that He might reconcile them both to God in one body through the cross, thereby putting to death the enmity. And He came and preached peace to you who were far off and to those who were near. For through Him we both have access by one Spirit to the Father" (Ephesians 2:13-14, 16-18).*

> *"For if when we were enemies we were reconciled to God through the death of His Son, much more, having been reconciled, we shall we be saved by His life" (Romans 5:10).*

> *". . . God was in Christ reconciling the world to Himself, not imputing their tresspasses to them . . ." (2 Corinthians 5:19).*

2. Christ as Our Priest Makes Intercession for Us

Our eternal security rests on the fact that the risen Lord Jesus Christ has the power of an endless life (Hebrews 7:16) to keep us saved for eternity. In this sense He makes intercession for us in His role as our Great High Priest.

> *"But He, because He lives forever, has an unchangeable priesthood. Therefore He is also able to save to the uttermost those who come to God through Him, since He always lives to make intercession for them" (Hebrews 7:24-25).*

> *"Who is he who condemns? It is Christ who died, and furthermore who is also risen, who is even at the right hand of God, who also makes intercession for us" (Romans 8:34).*

Christ as King

There is much said in Scripture about the kingship of Jesus Christ.

1. When He Was on Earth the First Time, He Was Announced as a King

> *"Now after Jesus was born in Bethlehem of Judea, in the days of Herod the king, behold, wise men from the East came to Jerusalem, saying, 'Where is He who has been born King of the Jews? For we have seen His star in the East and have come to worship Him'" (Matthew 2:1-2).* See also John 1:49.

When John the Baptist began preaching, he proclaimed that the kingdom of God was "at hand," that is, right in their midst. The Lord Jesus proclaimed the same message. In His public entry into Jerusalem toward the close of His earthly ministry, Christ formally offered Himself as the King, in fulfillment of Old Testament prophecy.

> *"All this was done that it might be fulfilled which was spoken by the prophet, saying, 'Tell the daughter of Zion, "Behold, your King is coming to you, lowly, and sitting on a donkey, a colt, the foal of a donkey"'" (Matthew 21:4-5).*

He was rejected by the nation of Israel and was crucified with the charge for His execution being, "King of the Jews" (John 19:19-22), which was, of course, true.

"He came to His own, and His own did not receive Him" (John 1:11).

2. Christ Is the Head of the Church

Anticipating His rejection, the Lord Jesus declared His purpose—to build a company of people He called the *church*.

> *"And I also say to you that you are Peter, and on this rock [Peter's confession that Jesus was the promised Redeemer] I will build My church, and the gates of Hades shall not prevail against it" (Matthew 16:18).*

This company would be open to all to join, by their common faith in Christ:

> *"There is neither Jew nor Greek, there is neither slave nor free, there is neither male nor female, for you are all one in Christ Jesus" (Galatians 3:28).*

While the Bible doesn't call Christ the "King of the church," He *is* called its "Head." It is evident that He is Sovereign over everyone who belongs to Him. He is the Lord who is to be obeyed.

> *"And He [God] put all things under His [Christ's] feet and gave Him to be head over all things to the church, which is His body, the fullness of Him who fills all in all" (Ephesians 1:22-23).*

3. Christ Is Coming Again to the Earth to Set Up His Kingdom

This is God's purpose as expressed in many prophecies in both the Old and New Testaments.

> *"And the LORD shall be king over all the earth. In that day it shall be—'The LORD is one' and His name one" (Zechariah 14:9).*

Describing the glorious return of Christ to earth, the book of Revelation says: "Now out of His mouth goes a sharp sword, that with it He should strike the nations. And He Himself will rule them with a rod of iron. He Himself treads the winepress of the fierceness and wrath of Almighty God. And He has on His robe and on His thigh a name written: KING OF KINGS and LORD OF LORDS" (Revelation 19:15-16). See also Revelation 11:15 and Daniel 7:13-14.

Christ will return to reign as King of kings for 1000 years. In the time of His kingdom, there will be righteousness, peace, and prosperity over all the earth.

> *"The wolf and the lamb shall feed together, the lion shall eat straw like the ox. 'They shall not hurt nor destroy in all My holy mountain,' says the L*ORD*" (Isaiah 65:25).* See also Isaiah 11:6-9 and Ezekiel 34:24-26.

During the millennial kingdom, Christ will be acknowledged by all as King of kings and Lord of lords. It is said that on one occasion when Handel's *Messiah* was being sung before Queen Victoria, she rose to her feet and took the crown from her head in reverence to the One whom the oratorio acclaims King of kings and Lord of lords.

In Christ as Prophet, we have the message and will of God revealed to us. In Christ as Priest, we have pardon and acceptance with God. In Christ as King, we have eventual deliverance from all enemies, even Satan himself. In Christ, therefore, we are complete.

Writing to the local church at Colossae, Paul said, "And you are complete in Him, who is the head of all principality and power" (Colossians 2:10).

Let's Sum Up Again

One of God's indictments of humanity reads like this: "Although they knew God, they did not glorify Him as God, nor were thankful, but became futile in their thoughts, and their foolish hearts were darkened" (Romans 1:21).

As you study the truths God has revealed, you either affirm them or reject them. Test yourself to see how you are relating these truths to your life. Be strictly honest and mentally answer each statement Yes or No.

Lesson 5—Man is a fallen creature: I know this is true because I can detect the working of sin in my own life.

Lesson 6—"The wages of sin is death." After death, comes the judgment. I believe that God is holy and that He punishes sin. If I do not embrace Jesus Christ as my Savior, I will be punished for my sins after death.

Lesson 7—Jesus Christ is the Son of God. He became a man in order to become the Savior of sinners. I believe that the Lord Jesus Christ came into the world to save sinners. I am a sinner.

Lesson 8—The Lord Jesus is God's Prophet, Priest, and King. I need the Lord Jesus Christ to reveal to me God's way of salvation. I also need Him to be my Advocate in God's presence. I need Him to rule my life as King.

You should be able to answer Yes to all these questions. If you cannot do this, you should go back over the lesson and ask God to help you apply the truths to your own life. These truths must be related to your life if you are to know their real meaning.

CHAPTER

9

WHAT THE BIBLE SAYS ABOUT THE HOLY SPIRIT

The Holy Spirit Is a Person of the Godhead

The Holy Spirit is one of the three persons of the Godhead. He is not a mere influence, as claimed by some false teachers. From what we read in the Scriptures of His personality, the following are particularly striking:

1. His Names Imply Personality as Well as Deity

He is linked with the Father and the Son in such passages as the baptismal "formula" (Matthew 28:19) and one of Paul's benedictions (2 Corinthians 13:14).

He is called "the Spirit of the Lord" (2 Corinthians 3:18); "the eternal Spirit" (Hebrews 9:14); "the Spirit of God" (Genesis 1:2); "the Spirit of Christ" (Romans 8:9); "the Spirit of truth" (John 15:26). These are typical of the titles the Scriptures use to convey that the Holy Spirit is a person, one with the Father and the Son.

(The word *Spirit* is more appropriate in modern English than *Ghost*, which occurs often in the King James Version of the Bible and is still retained in many hymns.)

2. Personal Pronouns Are Used in Reference to Him

No one would think of referring to the Father or to the Son as "it"; yet many people say "it" in reference to the Holy Spirit. This is partly due to poor translations of pronouns in the King James Version of the Bible (compare Romans 8:16, 26 in the KJV and the NKJV).

The masculine personal pronouns used in the Bible clearly show the personality of the Holy Spirit. Consider the words of the Lord Jesus concerning the Holy Spirit in John chapters 14–16; this is correctly translated in the English version by the personal pronoun "He" (John 14:16-17, 26; 15:26; 16:8, 13).

3. His Words and Deeds Prove His Personality

Only persons think, speak, and act. The words and deeds ascribed to the Holy Spirit in the Bible could not have been spoken or performed by an impersonal force or influence.

    a. He spoke to men in ancient times (Acts 1:16; Hebrews 3:7).

    b. He performed miracles (Acts 2:4; 8:39).

    c. He appointed "overseers" to "be shepherds of the church of God . . ." (Acts 20:28).

    d. He guided the apostles and their fellow laborers in their ministry (Acts 11:12; 13:2; 16:6-7).

    e. "The Spirit *Himself* bears witness with our spirit that we are children of God" (Romans 8:16).

    f. "The Spirit *Himself* makes intercession for us . . ." (Romans 8:26).

4. Man's Attitude Toward Him Evidences His Personality

    a. The Lord Jesus said that the Holy Spirit could be blasphemed against (Mark 3:29) and resisted (Acts 7:51) by the unregenerate.

    b. Christians can grieve Him (Ephesians 4:30), quench Him (1 Thessalonians 5:19), or be filled with Him (Ephesians 5:18).

The Holy Spirit Wrote the Bible Through Godly Men of Old

It was through the active work of the Holy Spirit that God produced the Scriptures (2 Timothy 3:16).

> *"For prophecy never came by the will of man, but holy men of God spoke as they were moved by the Holy Spirit"* (2 Peter 1:21). See also 2 Samuel 23:2.

The Holy Spirit Convicts the World of Sin, of Righteousness, and of Judgment (John 16:8-11)

The Holy Spirit convicts the world of sin with respect to its attitude to Christ—that its abiding refusal to believe in Him will result in permanent condemnation. The Holy Spirit convicts the world that the righteousness we need to be acceptable to God is found only in Christ, and that Christ has provided that to us at Calvary, where God condemned sin in the flesh (Romans 8:3-4).

Although physical pain is not pleasant, we are generally thankful for it because it signals something is wrong in our body. We need to address the cause if we want to be rid of the pain. How much more thankful we ought to be that the Holy Spirit convicts us of our inability to save ourselves (our sinful nature) and of our personal offences against our holy Creator God (our sins), so that we can take measures to be "cured." (And thank God that One does exist with the power to cure us of our sin!)

The Holy Spirit Regenerates the Sinner

In Acts 16:14 we read this about the conversion of a Greek woman named Lydia: "The Lord opened her heart to heed the things spoken by Paul." Romans 10:10 in the Holman Christian Standard Bible says, "So faith comes from what is heard, and what is heard comes through the message about Christ." The Holy Spirit of God takes the message of the gospel and applies it, creating in the sinner a new mind to believe and a new heart to embrace and love the truth of God.

Jesus said to Nicodemus, "Most assuredly, I say to you, unless one is born again, he cannot see the kingdom of God. . . . Unless one is born of water and [or, even] the Spirit, he cannot enter the kingdom of God" (John 3:3, 5; see also John 3:6-8).

> "And if anyone does not have the Spirit of Christ, he is not His" (Romans 8:9).
>
> "He [God] saved us through the washing of regeneration . . . by the Holy Spirit" (Titus 3:5).

In other words, the Holy Spirit does for the soul something similar to what the nurse does for the patient. Medicine exists that will make the sick person better, but it is not where the person can get it. In order to get a dosage of the medicine, the nurse must take it to the sick person and administer it.

What's more, the very moment that you and I were born again by the Spirit of God and the word preached about Christ, at that moment the Holy Spirit baptized (immersed) us into the church—we then became members of the body of Christ, intimately identified with it spiritually. (That is why we as believers do not *seek* the baptism of the Spirit, for we have already received it.)

> *"For we were all baptized by one Spirit into the body—whether Jews or Greeks, slave or free—and we were all given the one Spirit to drink" (1 Corinthians 12:13).*

Not only does the Holy Spirit regenerate us at the moment we believe in Christ, and at the same moment baptize us into the body of Christ. He also comes into us to indwell us forever, "And I will pray the Father, and He will give you another Helper, that He may abide with you forever—the Spirit of truth, whom the world cannot receive, because it neither sees Him nor knows Him; but you know Him, for He dwells with you and will be in you" (John 14:16-17). He also seals us, thus indicating God's ownership and our eternal security (Ephesians 1:13).

The Holy Spirit is referred to by Paul as "the guarantee of our inheritance" (Ephesians 1:14). Thus, He becomes the "token pledge" of heaven's joys. The blessings of His presence within us are proof that there is more to come.

All of these ministries of the Holy Spirit—regeneration, baptism, indwelling, and sealing—are accomplished once and for all when the sinner believes.

Let's pause and read again the Scriptures we have already noted in this lesson: Ephesians 4:30; 1 Thessalonians 5:19; Ephesians 5:18. It is tragically true that many who have been born again quench and grieve the Holy Spirit of God in a multitude of ways, even though we have been expressly commanded to be filled with the Spirit. To heed this command we must walk in the Spirit (Galatians 5:25), obey God fully, and claim His promise of power to overcome sin; we do this by Bible study, prayer, and love for Him who "did not spare His own Son, but delivered Him up for us all" (Romans 8:32).

The Holy Spirit Indwells the Believer and Empowers Him for Service

The indwelling of the Holy Spirit is permanent. The filling of the Spirit is the ministry of the Spirit by which He actually empowers the believer to fulfill God's purpose for him or her (Ephesians 2:10). We can interrupt and hinder this ministry by sin in our lives. For this reason, we need to put away sin and yield to the Spirit repeatedly to allow Him to do His work.

As believers in Christ, we need to remember that our bodies have now been set apart, because they are a dwelling place of God. "Do you not know that your body is the temple of the Holy Spirit who is in you, whom you have from God, and you are not your own? For you were bought at a price; therefore glorify God in your body" (1 Corinthians 6:19-20).

The indwelling Holy Spirit is the believer's comforter, teacher, and guide. "But the Helper, the Holy Spirit, whom the Father will send in My name, He will teach you all things . . ." (John 14:26; see also John 15:26; 16:12-15). Although these promises were made by the Lord Jesus specifically to His disciples, they still apply to us in principle today.

As our Teacher, the Spirit of God enlightens our minds in the knowledge of Christ. "Now we have received, not the spirit of the world, but the Spirit who is from God, that we might know the things that have been freely given to us by God" (1 Corinthians 2:12). There is a whole world of important spiritual truth we need to learn. Without the Holy Spirit revealing this truth, we could not understand and enjoy Jesus Christ. Moreover, the Spirit empowers us for service:

> *"We [Paul and Timothy] do not cease to pray for you, and to ask that . . . you may walk worthy of the Lord, . . . being fruitful in every good work . . . strengthened with all might according to His glorious power" (Colossians. 1:9-11).*

Let us remember that it is one thing to *know* the truth, and it is another thing to *act upon* it and *obey* it. But the gracious Spirit of God does not leave His work of mercy half-done. Not only does He enlighten our minds, He also renews our wills. He shows us the truth, and He gives us the disposition to love it. We sometimes grow weary of doing good. Then the Holy Spirit comes to our relief, strengthens our faith, encourages our hearts, and empowers us to do the will of God. Then we realize our utter dependence upon Him and can say with the prophet of old, "'Not by might nor by power, but by My Spirit,' says the LORD of hosts" (Zechariah 4:6).

CHAPTER

10

WHAT THE BIBLE SAYS ABOUT FAITH AND REPENTANCE

To depend on our good works in order to get right with God and earn eternal life is a false hope. It has been said that the Ten Commandments, which epitomize God's perfect and holy standard, are like the ten links of a chain by which a man might hang suspended over a cliff—only one link needs to be broken to cause the man's death.

In the same vein, James says, "For whoever shall keep the whole law, and yet stumble in one point, he is guilty of all" (James 2:10). For example, if you have coveted something that belongs to someone else, you have broken the Ten Commandments. Nowhere in the Bible does it teach good works is a condition for salvation. In fact, faith as the sole means of justification with God is taught in both the Old and the New Testaments:

> "*The just shall live by his faith*" *(Habakkuk 2:4).* Literally, this reads "The just [or righteous] by faith shall live."
>
> "*But that no one is justified by the law in the sight of God is evident, for 'the just shall live by faith'*" *(Galatians 3:11).*
>
> "*Believe on the Lord Jesus Christ, and you will be saved*" *(Acts 16:31).*

Some people speak of different steps that the sinner must take in order to be saved, citing passages of Scripture in which repentance is mentioned as though it were a separate step in addition to faith. When the gospel message is properly presented and understood, it is evident that the spiritual exercises of faith and repentance are inseparable. They are two sides of the same coin.

Although faith and repentance cannot be separated in practice, we can make an artificial separation or analysis for the purpose of studying what they are.

Faith

1. Saving Faith Is Receiving Jesus Christ

In salvation, we give nothing and we receive everything. Our hearts are corrupt and therefore not acceptable to God. Our hearts must be cleansed from sin before we can enter His family and enjoy His life. This cleansing is brought about when we exercise personal faith in the person and work of Christ on the cross for us, recognizing its sufficiency for us.

> *"But as many as received Him, to them He gave the right to become children of God, to those who believe in His name" (John 1:12).*

> *"But you were washed, but you were sanctified, but you were justified in the name of the Lord Jesus Christ and by the Spirit of our God" (1 Corinthians 6:11).*

2. Saving Faith Is Receiving and Resting upon Jesus Christ

To rest upon Christ means to be no longer anxious about our eternal destiny or acceptability to our Creator God. It is to believe that God loved you enough to send His Son to die for you, to be confident that God Himself provided "the redemption that is in Christ Jesus" and that He is "just and the justifier of the one who has faith in Jesus" (Romans 3:24, 26). The result of such a step of faith is peace with God and peace for the soul.

> *"Therefore, having been justified by faith, we have peace with God through our Lord Jesus Christ" (Romans 5:1).*

> *"In this the love of God was manifested toward us, that God has sent His only begotten Son into the world, that we might live through Him.... Love has been perfected among us in this: that we may have boldness in the day of judgment; ... There is no fear in love; but perfect love [that is, God's love] casts out [our] fear, because fear involves torment. But he who fears has not been made perfect in love" (1 John 4:9, 17-18).*

3. Saving Faith Is Receiving and Resting upon Jesus Christ Alone

We have not exercised true faith in Jesus Christ if we trust partly in Him and partly in ourselves. God will not permit any partnership with Himself in the work of salvation. Good works should *follow* salvation as an evidence of the genuine work done by the Spirit in us, and out of appreciation for our salvation. Our works cannot take the place of our Savior's work.

> *"For by grace you have been saved through faith, and that not of yourselves; it is the gift of God, not of works, lest anyone should boast"* (Ephesians 2:8-9).

> *"Not by works of righteousness which we have done, but according to His mercy He saved us through the washing of regeneration and renewing of the Holy Spirit"* (Titus 3:5).

In the world of religion, people talk a lot about faith, "coming to faith," or having faith in many and varied things, even in themselves and their faith! Faith that results in forgiveness from God and salvation is faith that embraces and rests on Jesus Christ alone.

4. Saving Faith Is Receiving and Resting upon Jesus Christ Alone as He Is Offered to Us in the Gospel

Our own thoughts about Christ are not enough. We have no authority for trusting in human ideas about Christ. What matters is *God's* view about His Son and His saving work. Only the Bible can teach us clearly who the Lord Jesus Christ is and what He has done for us.

> *"When He [Jesus] had been baptized . . . suddenly a voice came from heaven saying, 'This is My beloved Son, in whom I am well pleased'"* (Matthew 3:16-17).

> *"[God] has in these last days spoken to us by His Son . . . who being the brightness of His glory and the express image of His person, and upholding all things by the word of His power, when He had by Himself purged our sins, sat down at the right hand of the Majesty on high"* (Hebrews 1:2-3).

> *". . . the gospel of God . . . concerning His Son Jesus Christ our Lord, who was born of the seed of David according to the flesh, and declared to be the Son of God with power according to the*

Spirit of holiness, by the resurrection from the dead" (Romans 1:1-4).

Repentance

1. Repentance—a Change of Mind Toward God

The word *repentance* means "a change of mind," a change of purpose. Repentance is well illustrated in the Gospels by Zacchaeus the tax collector (Luke 18:13), the prodigal son (Luke 15:17-21), and the son who first refused to obey his father's command to work in his vineyard "but afterward . . . regretted it and went" (Matthew 21:29).

In relation to salvation, repentance comprises a turning away from sin—a definite change of mind toward God as a result of genuine heart conviction of the sin that offends Him. Paul preached to both Jews and Gentiles, saying "that they should repent, turn to God, and do works befitting repentance" (Acts 26:20).

Isaiah urged the rebellious nation of Judah: "Let the wicked forsake his way, and the unrighteous man his thoughts; let him return to the LORD, and He will have mercy on him; and to our God, for He will abundantly pardon" (Isaiah 55:7).

Some think that repentance is the same as being sorry for sin, but this is by no means true. Sorrow for sin in itself is not repentance. A child will say he's sorry in order to escape punishment, but if he is not truly repentant for his wrongdoing, he will commit the same misdeed soon afterward. One who is truly sorry for sin agrees with God that his sin is an abominable thing that God hates and turns away from sinning against Him—that person is repentant.

> "If we confess our sins, He is faithful and just to forgive us our sins and to cleanse us from all unrighteousness . . . My little children, these things I write to you, so that you may not sin. And if anyone sins, we have an Advocate with the Father, Jesus Christ the righteous" (1 John 1:9; 2:1).

A genuine Christian will characteristically be sorry for any sins he commits because he knows that it offends his Lord and that Jesus Christ suffered and died because of that sin. He will not want to commit that sin again. What's more, he will seek to live so close to the Savior that he will confess all known sin—not just a particular disobedience—instantly, just as quickly as he will be pardoned by the God of forgiving love.

2. The Necessity for Repentance

Jesus Himself declared the priority of repentance. At the beginning of His earthly public ministry, speaking to the nation of Israel, He stated plainly: "I tell you . . . unless you repent you will all likewise perish" (Luke 13:3). His message was, "Repent, for the kingdom of heaven is at hand!" (Matthew 3:2). And after He rose from the dead He said to His disciples, "Thus it is written, and thus it was necessary for the Christ to suffer and to rise from the dead the third day, and that repentance and remission of sins should be preached in His name to all nations, beginning at Jerusalem" (Luke 24:46-47).

Following are some of the inspired words the apostles spoke concerning the necessity for repentance with respect to salvation:

> "Repent therefore and be converted, that your sins may be blotted out, so that times of refreshing may come from the presence of the Lord" (Acts 3:19).

> "Truly these times of ignorance God overlooked, but now commands all men everywhere to repent" (Acts 17:30).

> "Your faith toward God has gone out, so that we do not need to say anything. . . . For [the believers in Achaia] themselves declare . . . how you turned to God from idols to serve the living and true God" (1 Thessalonians 1:8-9).

> "The Lord is not slack concerning His promise, as some count slackness, but is longsuffering toward us, not willing that any should perish but that all should come to repentance" (2 Peter 3:9).

We have seen that the only thing necessary to salvation is faith in the finished work of the Lord Jesus Christ. Any person who recognizes their need of salvation will logically repent of their sins in the process of putting their faith in Christ, because it was for those sins that the Savior suffered and died.

CHAPTER

11

WHAT THE BIBLE SAYS ABOUT THE CHRISTIAN'S HERITAGE

When God forgives our sins, figuratively speaking He removes them "as far as the east is from the west"; they will never bar us from being rightly related to our Creator God again (Psalm 103:12). But forgiveness of our sins is just one of the immeasurable riches God bestows on the believer both now and in the future life.

The apostle Paul stated in Ephesians 1:3 that God has "blessed us with every spiritual blessing in the heavenly places *in Christ*" (emphasis added). In this lesson we will look further at some of the spiritual blessings that are the privilege and portion of every Christian.

In This Life

The blessings related to our redemption may be summarized in five significant words: justification, adoption, and sanctification, security, and assurance.

1. Justification

The Bible teaches us that justification is a judicious act of God whereby He declares the sinner to be righteous (and therefore acceptable to Him) when the sinner places his faith in Jesus Christ to save him.

> *"And by Him [Christ] everyone who believes is justified from all things from which you could not be justified by the law of Moses" (Acts 13:39).*

> *"Therefore, having been justified by faith, we have peace with God through our Lord Jesus Christ" (Romans 5:1).*

It is obvious that a righteous God could not do this apart from some righteous ground for His declaration. That righteous ground is the sacrificial death of the Lord Jesus for us.

> *"He made Him who knew no sin to be sin for us, that we might become the righteousness of God in Him" (2 Corinthians 5:21).*

The Scriptures teach that we are "justified . . . by His grace" (Romans 3:24); "justified by His blood" (Romans 5:9); and "justified by faith" (Romans 3:28; 5:1).

These expressions teach us that (a) God's grace is the source of our justification; (b) Christ's death is the ground, or basis, of it; and (c) our faith is the channel, or means, through which our justification is appropriated.

God declares the believing sinner righteous in His sight because he is identified with God's condemnation of sin when He judged Christ while He hung on the cross; he therefore partakes of the benefits of His death. Not only are his sins paid for and forgiven, but God graciously treats him as though he had not sinned. We are "accepted in the Beloved" (Ephesians 1:6). Indeed, God sees him "in Christ," with Christ's positive righteousness reckoned to him. The sinner is accounted righteous not through any righteousness of his own, but because he is now "clothed" in Christ's righteousness. The believer is now no longer an enemy of God; rather, he is at peace with Him (Romans 5:9-11).

2. Adoption

In today's use, adoption is the act of making another person's child one's own. The word *adoption* is used five times in the English Bible. One of these occurrences refers to the completion of our redemption when our bodies are resurrected (Romans 8:23); another refers to Israel's favored position in Old Testament times (Romans 9:4). The other three uses of the word have to do with the believer's position, or place of privilege, in God's household.

> *"For you did not receive the spirit of bondage again to fear, but you received the Spirit of adoption by whom we cry out, 'Abba, Father'" (Romans 8:15).*

> *". . . Having predestined us to adoption as sons by Jesus Christ to Himself, according to the good pleasure of His will" (Ephesians 1:5).*

> "But when the fullness of the time had come, God sent forth His Son, born of a woman, born under the law, to redeem those who were under the law, that we might receive the adoption as sons. And because you are sons, God has sent forth the Spirit of His Son into your hearts, crying out, 'Abba, Father!' Therefore you are no longer a slave but a son, and if a son, then an heir of God through Christ" (Galatians 4:4-7).

From these passages it is apparent that the scriptural doctrine of adoption involves much more than the modern use of the word. In the original Greek word, adoption meant "placing as a son"—that is, investing any young person of a wealthy person's choice with the privileges and responsibilities of sonship, usually relating to inheritance.

The question is often raised: If we are *born* into the family of God, why do we need to be *adopted*? The answer is this: we become *children of God* by the new birth, and *sons of God* by adoption. (Regeneration and adoption take place at the same time.) Through regeneration, or the new birth, we enter God's family (John 1:12-13); this is a matter of relationship. Adoption does not have to do with our relationship with God, but with our standing in His family as full-grown sons.

If you carefully read Galatians chapters 3 and 4 you will see that the whole point of the doctrine of adoption is that, positionally, every believer in Christ is an adult son in God's family. Sadly, many believers live as "babes in Christ" (1 Corinthians 3:1) experientially and do not take advantage of their standing as full-grown sons. One of the ministries of the Holy Spirit is to impress on us the dignity of our position and to help us live "royally" in light of it.

> "You are all sons of God through faith in Christ Jesus" (Galatians 3:26).

3. Sanctification

In each of the original languages in which the Bible was written (the Old Testament in Hebrew, and the New Testament in Greek), the word translated "sanctify" has the root meaning of "to set apart." The words "sanctify," "sanctification," "saint," "holy," and "holiness" are all related to one another in meaning. When God sanctifies a person, He sets that person apart to Himself. This involves, of course, the essential truth that the person is set apart from sin.

There are three aspects of our sanctification:

a. Positional Sanctification

". . . We have been sanctified through the offering of the body of Jesus Christ once for all" (Hebrews 10:10).

In our standing before God, all believers have been sanctified—made completely holy and pure. We can see this in the case of the Corinthian Christians, who were addressed as "sanctified in Christ Jesus, called to be saints [holy ones]" (1 Corinthians 1:2) even though their lives were far from what God wanted them to be. In other words, although a Christian may not always act like God's child, he still is one.

b. Experiential, or Practical, Sanctification

In the practical, experiential sense, we who are believers are *being* sanctified. God's purpose is that we be conformed more and more to the likeness of Jesus Christ.

"For whom He foreknew, He also predestined to be conformed to the image of His Son" (Romans 8:29).

In this life, God does not remove our sin nature when we trust Christ for salvation, so we still have the capacity to sin. However, our positional sanctification ought to inspire us to conduct our lives to reflect our position. There are at least two conditions a believer must meet to open the way for the Holy Spirit to work in his life:

1. Yieldedness to God . . .

"I beseech you therefore, brethren, by the mercies of God, that you present your bodies a living sacrifice, holy, acceptable to God, which is your reasonable service. And do not be conformed to this world, but be transformed by the renewing of your mind, that you may prove what is that good and acceptable and perfect will of God" (Romans 12:1-2).

Only as we intentionally yield ourselves to God, giving ourselves over to Him completely, can the Holy Spirit produce His fruit in our lives (Galatians 5:16-25). It is possible to be a Christian without being yielded to God, but it is not possible to be a Spirit-filled Christian without surrendering to Him.

> *"And do not present your members [like your mind, tongue, hands, etc] as instruments of unrighteousness to sin, but present yourselves to God as being alive from the dead, and your members as instruments of righteousness to God"* (Romans 6:13).

2. Faith . . .

As believers we must depend on the Holy Spirit moment by moment for victory over temptation. We must believe that Christ can and will live His life through us.

> *"Walk in the Spirit, and you shall not fulfill the lust of the flesh"* (Galatians 5:16).

Paul testified, "I have been crucified with Christ; it is no longer I who live, but Christ lives in me; and the life which I now live in the flesh I live by faith in the Son of God, who loved me and gave Himself for me" (Galatians 2:20).

c. Ultimate Sanctification

We as believers will be entirely sanctified at the return of the Lord Jesus Christ (1 Thessalonians 5:23). At that time our experience will be in perfect harmony with our position. This is a future benefit rather than a present one.

> *"Beloved, now we are children of God, and it has not yet been revealed what we shall be, but we know that when He is revealed, we shall be like Him, for we shall see Him as He is"* (1 John 2:2).

4. Security

Even though we do still sin, God keeps us saved. Christ promised that His sheep would *never* perish but be secure eternally, safe in His Father's hand (John 10:27-28).

> *"Now to Him who is able to keep you from stumbling, and to present you faultless before the presence of His glory with exceeding joy, to God our Savior, who alone is wise, be glory and majesty, dominion and power, both now and forever. Amen"* (Jude 24-25).

Time and again in Scripture the Christian is promised eternal life when he believes in Christ (e.g. John 3:16); and life that is eternal cannot be lost. While it is possible for a genuine Christian to sometimes doubt his salvation, understanding the doctrines of justification, adoption, and sanctification—as well as appreciating them—help a Christian to have a growing confidence that he has truly been saved, and that his salvation is secure for all eternity.

5. Assurance

A child develops an assurance of belonging to a family by a number of ways. He can read what is written on his birth certificate; he may note his resemblance to his parents; he will listen to them tell him he is their child; and he experiences their practical love for him day by day. In the same way, our assurance is based on what is written in God's Word (1 John 5:13), our growing likeness to Christ (1 John 3:10), the witness of the Spirit telling us we are God's children (Romans 8:15-16), and our ongoing walk with Him (Ephesians 5:1-8).

When we realize that God has forgiven our sins and made us fit for heaven, that He has made us His children with all the privileges of sonship, and that He has set us apart for Himself and is causing us to grow in godliness, how can we doubt His love for us? And since there is no doubt of His love for us, what hinders us from having perfect peace and joy in our hearts all the time?

What's more, if God loves us, how can we keep from loving Him in return? If we love Him, shall we not obey Him? And if we obey Him, shall we not desire to be transformed into Christ's image, from one stage of glory to another (2 Corinthians 3:18)?

> *"Therefore, having these promises, beloved, let us cleanse ourselves from all filthiness of the flesh and spirit, perfecting holiness in the fear of God" (2 Corinthians 7:1).*

In the Life to Come

1. The Sting of Death Removed

As believers, we do not need to fear death, because its sting was removed when Christ died and rose again.

> *"Inasmuch then as the children have partaken of flesh and blood, He Himself likewise shared in the same, that through death He might destroy him who had the power of death, that is, the devil, and release those who through fear of death were all their lifetime subject to bondage"* (Hebrews 2:14-15).

> *"'O Death, where is your sting? O Hades, where is your victory?' The sting of death is sin, and the strength of sin is the law. But thanks be to God, who gives us the victory through our Lord Jesus Christ"* (1 Corinthians 15:55-57).

> *"For we know that if our earthly house, this tent, is destroyed, we have a building from God, a house not made with hands, eternal in the heavens. For in this we groan, earnestly desiring to be clothed with our habitation which is from heaven"* (2 Corinthians 5:1-2).

2. "Absent from the body . . . present with the Lord" (2 Corinthians 5:8)

At death, the believer's spirit goes to be with Christ, even as He said to the penitent thief, "Today you will be with Me in paradise" (Luke 23:43). Paul described his desire to depart and be with Christ as "far better" than continuing in this earthly life (Philippians 1:23).

While the spirits of the redeemed are with Christ, their bodies rest in the grave until the first resurrection (1 Thessalonians 4:13-18; Revelation 20:4-6).

3. To Be "raised in glory" (1 Corinthians 15:43)

When the Lord Jesus Christ comes again, He will bring forth the spirits of believers with Him and will call forth our bodies from the grave. Then we will live forever, completely redeemed, in glorified, resurrected bodies.

a. "We shall be like Him" (1 John 3:2)

God's purpose of conforming us to the image of His Son will be perfectly fulfilled (Romans 8:29).

> *"For our citizenship is in heaven, from which we also eagerly wait for the Savior, the Lord Jesus Christ, who will transform our lowly body that it may be conformed to His glorious body,*

according to the working by which He is able even to subdue all things to Himself" (Philippians 3:20-21).

b. Our Resurrection Bodies Will Be Real

The glorified bodies of believers will be like Christ's, and His risen body was real—a body of "flesh and bones" (Luke 24:39).

First Corinthians chapter 15 is the central passage on the resurrection, showing us that we will be the same, yet not the same—the same in individual identity, yet changed in constituent particles and appearance.

c. We Shall Know the Fullness of Blessing in Spirit, Soul, and Body

> *"He will wipe every tear from their eyes. There shall be no more death, nor sorrow, nor crying. There shall be no more pain, for the former things have passed away"* (Revelation 21:4).

d. We Shall Be "to the praise of His glory" (Ephesians 1:12; 3:10-11)

The purity of heaven will not admit the presence of anything that is sinful or defiling.

> *"That He [Christ] might present her [the church] to himself a glorious church, not having spot or wrinkle or any such thing blemish, but that she should be holy and without blemish"* (Ephesians 5:27).

> *"But there shall by no means enter it anything that defiles, or causes an abomination or a lie, but only those who are written in the Lamb's Book of Life"* (Revelation 21:27).

The blessing to come to believers can be summed up in the full enjoyment of God forever and ever. Try to imagine a life where the very thought of an eventual end to things is taken away, where life will simply go on and on. Add to that the prospect of being engaged in the blissful occupation of serving God in His presence throughout all eternity!

> *"His servants shall serve Him. They shall see His face"* (Revelation 22:3-4).

The psalmist said it well: "You will show me the path of life; in Your presence is fullness of joy; at Your right hand are pleasures forevermore" (Psalm 16:11).

CHAPTER

12

WHAT THE BIBLE SAYS ABOUT LIVING THE CHRISTIAN LIFE

Once a person becomes a child of God, he ought to grow in that new life. We have seen previously that God graces every believer with full rights as an adult son as soon as he believes in Christ, but in his Christian experience, every believer starts as a spiritual baby.

Peter exhorted some first-century believers to "grow in the grace and knowledge of our Lord Jesus Christ" (2 Peter 3:18). Now we want to consider some of the means that God uses to bring about our spiritual growth. God has given us certain helps that we may know Him better, overcome sin in our lives, be channels of blessing to others, and become more and more like Christ. Why is it that some Christians never grow, or make so little progress in their spiritual experience? Because they neglect the means of growth that God has provided. Read in this connection 1 Corinthians 3:1-4 and Hebrews 5:11-14.

The most necessary means for growing spiritually are: (1) the study and application of the Word of God; (2) the practice of prayer; (3) the assembling of ourselves together; and (4) practicing the ordinances given by God.

The Study of the Word of God

Of first importance among the God-given helps to Christian growth is His own written Word.

> "Like newborn babies, crave pure spiritual milk, so that by it you may grow up in your salvation" (1 Peter 2:2).

Peter's readers were not necessarily new believers ("babes in the faith"); *all* Christians should crave the spiritual nourishment found in the Bible. In the everyday affairs of life we know that we cannot master any subject without careful study; however, many Christians imagine that God in some mysterious way will give them spiritual knowledge without them studying the Bible. Here are some suggestions of ways in which we should study God's Word.

1. We Should Study the Word with Diligence

The people of Berea who heard Paul's preaching are an example of those who search the Bible regularly and diligently.

> *"These [Bereans] received the word with all readiness, and searched the Scriptures daily to find out whether these things [what Paul had taught them from the Old Testament] were so" (Acts 17:11).*

Unless we do at least this much, our study will not be very honoring to God or very helpful to us.

> *"Be diligent to present yourself approved to God, a worker who does not need to be ashamed, rightly dividing the word of truth" (2 Timothy 2:15).*

> *"I have more understanding than all my teachers, for Your testimonies are my meditation" (Psalm 119:99).*

2. We Should Study the Bible with Humility of Spirit

We should receive the Word humbly, with teachable spirits. Our prayer and attitude should be like the psalmist's:

> *"Establish Your word to Your servant, who is devoted to fearing You" (Psalm 119:38).*

> *"Therefore lay aside all filthiness and overflow of wickedness, and receive with meekness the implanted word, which is able to save your souls" (James 1:21).*

We must not be too proud to learn or to obey what we read. When we come to something in the Word that is beyond our understanding, we must purpose to believe it anyway. We also must resolve to obey God's

Word, even though doing so may be difficult and costly at times, and take discipline and effort.

3. We Should Study the Bible Prayerfully

We need God's help to understand His Word as we read it. We can pray as the psalmist did:

> "Open my eyes that I may see wonderful things in Your law" (Psalm 119:18).

The reason many people say they do not understand the Scriptures (and hence, are not interested in reading them) is that they do not ask God to be their Teacher.

> "And He [Jesus] opened their [the disciples'] understanding, that they might comprehend the Scriptures" (Luke 24:45). See also Luke 24:25-32.

In John 14:26, Jesus promised His disciples that the Holy Spirit would teach them when He came, and His promise is true for us in principle today as well. See also John 15:28 and 16:12-15.

4. We Should Study the Word with Appreciation for Its Value

For centuries, the only Bible available to believers was chained to a desk in the village church. Frequently, Christians had to pay for the privilege of having a Bible to read for even a short time. Even today, many Christians in some parts of the world have little or no access to a Bible. Let us never forget what a valuable possession a Bible is! The psalmist's perspective was this:

> "The law of the LORD is perfect, converting the soul; the testimony of the LORD is sure, making wise the simple; . . . the judgments of the LORD are true and righteous altogether. more to be desired are they than gold, yea, than much fine gold; sweeter also than honey and the honeycomb" (Psalm 19:9-10).

The Practice of Prayer

Reading the Bible is hearing God talk to *us*; to grow as a Christian we must maintain communication from *our* side—we must talk to *Him*. This is prayer. Let us consider what prayer is.

1. Prayer Is the Soul's Adoration of God

David, who authored many psalms, said in a prayer recorded in 2 Samuel 7:22, "You are great, O Lord God. For there is none like You, nor is there any God besides You, according to all that we have heard with our ears."

Worship is the expression of our heart to God for who He is, His character. There are too many psalms that could be cited which can be classified as worship psalms, but read Psalms 92, 103, and 145 for samples of them. When we focus on worshiping God we are not making any requests of God at all; neither are we even praising or thanking Him for what He has done. Rather, we recite His attributes—His holiness, His power, His love, His greatness, and His wonderful goodness. Our souls are taken up entirely with the thought of Him, of what He is in Himself. This is adoration, and this is one part of prayer.

2. Prayer Is the Expression of Our Desires to God

Prayer is also making requests of God for what we think we need, and what we wish He would give us (or do for others). Jacob asked Him for food and clothing (Genesis 28:20), and so may we; but there are some things far more important than material needs. Paul thanked the Corinthians for praying for his physical safety (2 Corinthians 1:7-11). Our spiritual needs far outweigh our material needs, and we ought to recognize this fact in our praying as Paul did in his (e.g. Ephesians 1:15-23).

> *"If then you were raised with Christ, seek those things which are above, where Christ is, sitting at the right hand of God" (Colossians 3:1).*

3. Prayer Is Asking God for Things That Are in Accord with His Will

We cannot expect God to give us what is not best for us. This is one reason some of our prayers are not answered.

> *"You ask and do not receive, because you ask amiss, that you may spend it on your pleasures" (James 4:3).*

If we trust only in our own judgment, we cannot expect to know God's will for us. But He has told us much about His will in His written Word, and He has given us the Holy Spirit to help us.

Likewise the Spirit also helps in our weaknesses. For we do not know what we should pray for as we ought, but the Spirit Himself makes intercession for us with groanings which cannot be uttered. Now He who searches the hearts knows what the mind of the Spirit is, because He makes intercession for the saints according to the will of God" (Romans 8:26-27).

"Now this is the confidence that we have in Him, that if we ask anything according to His will, He hears us" (1 John 5:14).

4. Prayer Is Petitioning the Father in the Name of His Son, Jesus Christ

Our privilege of coming into God's presence and asking things of Him is only on the basis of what Christ has done to make our reception possible. When we pray to the Father, we should recognize we are doing so on Christ's authority and limit our requests to what we believe He Himself would ask for, for God's honor and glory.

"And whatever you ask in My name, that I will do, that the Father may be glorified in the Son" (John 14:13). See also John 14:14; 15:16; and 16:23-24.

5. Prayer Includes the Confession of Sin

We should be careful not to omit confession, for we always stand in need of it, and it helps to keep us humble and grateful before God.

"If I regard iniquity in my heart, the Lord will not hear" (Psalm 66:18).

"If we confess our sins, He is faithful and just to forgive us our sins and to cleanse us from all unrighteousness" (1 John 1:9).

6. Prayer Is Linked with the Thankful Acknowledgement of God's Mercies

It is selfish always to be asking God for blessings and never thanking Him for those already received. Ingratitude is such an "easy sin," and in human history one of the first steps away from God (Romans 1:21). We should continually pray,

"Bless the LORD, O my soul, and forget not all His benefits" (Psalm 103:2).

"Be anxious for nothing, but in everything by prayer and supplication, with thanksgiving, let your requests be made known to God" (Philippians 4:6).

7. Effectual Prayer Is Persevering—the Expression of Faith

Read Luke 11:5-13 and 18:1-8 for illustrations that Jesus gave His disciples of the truth expressed in the following passages:

"Assuredly, I say to you, if you have faith as a mustard seed, you will say to this mountain, 'Move from here to there,' and it will move; and nothing will be impossible for you" (Matthew 17:20).

"And whatever things you ask in prayer, believing, you will receive" (Matthew 21:22). See also 1 John 5:14-15.

"The prayer of a righteous man is powerful and effective" (James 5:16).

The Assembling of Ourselves Together

Fellowshiping with other believers is vital for Christian growth. Attending church, engaging in the public worship of God, listening to the Bible preaching and teaching, and serving with our God-given talents are means that God uses to grow us and to use us to bless others.

". . . not forsaking the assembling of ourselves together, as is the manner of some, but exhorting one another, and so much the more as you see the Day approaching" (Hebrews 10:25).

"One generation shall praise Your works to another, and shall declare Your mighty acts" (Psalm 145:4).

". . . Be filled with the Spirit, speaking to one another in psalms and hymns and spiritual songs, singing and making melody in your heart to the Lord" (Ephesians 5:18-19).

Observing the Ordinances Given by Christ

All who are truly converted are expected to obey our Lord's specific commands to be baptized and to regularly partake of the Lord's Supper. Both baptism and the Lord's Supper symbolize our salvation, and in practicing them we grow in our appreciation of what the Lord did for us.

1. What Is Baptism?

The word *baptism* means "immersion." In the process of being dipped or immersed in a liquid, a item becomes "identified" with it. For example, a piece of cloth dipped in purple dye will become purple. Being physically baptized is an outward expression of an inward, spiritual identification with Christ and publically announcing that one is a follower of His. In the early history of the church, Christians obeyed the Lord by being baptized after receiving Him as their Savior. In going down into the water we symbolically show that we have passed through death and burial with Christ (Romans 6:1-5). When we come up out of the water, we identify with Him in His resurrection. We are dead to the old life and raised to new life in Christ (Colossians 3:1-3).

Baptism does not save us! A sinner is regenerated only by the Holy Spirit who makes the guilty soul a "new creation" in Christ Jesus (2 Corinthians 5:17; 1 Peter 1:23).

Jesus gave this command to His apostles: "Go therefore and make disciples of all the nations, baptizing them in the name of the Father and of the Son and of the Holy Spirit" (Matthew 28:19).

> *"'Can anyone forbid water, that these should not be baptized who have received the Holy Spirit just as we have?'" And he [Peter] commanded them to be baptized in the name of the Lord" (Acts 10:47-48).*

2. What Is the Lord's Supper?

Whereas baptism is passive (in that it is carried out by a third party on a person to illustrate that salvation was done *for* us), the Lord's Supper is an ordinance in which we actively participate. Christ instituted the remembrance feast on the evening in which He was betrayed, the day before He was crucified:

> *"And He took bread, gave thanks and broke it, and gave it to them, saying, 'This is My body which is given for you; do this in remembrance of Me.' Likewise He also took the cup after supper, saying, 'This cup is the new covenant in My blood, which is shed for you'"(Luke 22:19-20).*

a. It Is a Memorial of Our Redemption by Christ's Death

Christ told His followers to carry out this simple act to remember His sacrificial death for us on the cross, where He suffered in His body at the hands of men and of God. When He appears in glory, we will no longer need to "remember" Him, for we will dwell in His presence forever!

> *"For as often as you eat this bread and drink this cup, you proclaim the Lord's death till He comes" (1 Corinthians 11:26).*

b. It Is a Sign of the Fellowship That We Have with Christ and with Fellow Believers in Him

People who sit down and eat together at the same table are generally friends. When we gather around the Lord's Table, we show to the world that not only are we one with Christ, but also one with one another. For this reason, the Scripture speaks of the Lord's Supper as the *Communion*.

> *"The cup of blessing which we bless, is it not the communion of the blood of Christ? The bread which we break, is it not the communion of the body of Christ? For we, though many, are one bread and one body; for we all partake of that one bread"* (1 Corinthians 10:16-17).

Since the Lord's Supper is simply a memorial and a sign, it is not Christ's literal body and blood that we consume. The elements of bread and wine are *symbols* of His body and blood. The concept of our "feeding" on Him, as taught in John 6, is a picture of our believing in Him for salvation (see vv. 35, 47-56).

In 1 Corinthians chapter 11, Christians are warned against partaking of the Lord's Supper "in an unworthy manner." We should examine our own hearts, confessing known sin, before doing so.

> *"But let a man examine himself and so let him eat of the bread and drink of the cup"* (1 Corinthians 11:28; cf. 1 Corinthians 11:20-34).

As we let the Holy Spirit apply to our hearts the lessons to be learned from these ways of growing as Christians—studying the Word of God, praying, meeting with other believers, and practicing the ordinances given by Christ—we must remember this: "And do not be conformed to this world, but be transformed by the renewing of your mind, that you may prove what is that good and acceptable and perfect will of God" (Romans 12:2).

Then at life's end, we should be able to say with Paul: "I have fought the good fight, I have finished the race, I have kept the faith. Finally, there is laid up for me the crown of righteousness, which the Lord, the righteous Judge, will give to me on that Day, and not to me only but also to all who have loved His appearing" (2 Timothy 4:7-8).

Let's Sum Up

Will a meal satisfy a hungry man if he only prepares it, serves it, and contemplates it? No! He must eat it. Will the truths of this course be of any practical value to you if you only read them, study them, and answer questions on them? No! You must apply them. Test yourself to see if you are putting them into practice. Check each statement Yes or No.

Lesson 9—The Holy Spirit is God. He is also a person, and it is He who imparts spiritual life to those who take Christ as their Savior. It is He who sustains that life once it has begun. I realize that unless the Holy Spirit lives in me, I am not a true Christian.

Lesson 10—Faith and repentance are two sides of the same coin. God demands both. I have turned from my own selfish and sinful ways. I have received the Lord Jesus Christ, by faith, as my Savior.

Lesson 11—The Christian has a glorious heritage. In this life he becomes a son of God when he takes Christ as his Lord and Savior, and he is expected to live accordingly. A glorious future awaits the believer in the life to come. Since believing in Christ I have begun to enjoy this heritage.

Lesson 12—Bible reading, prayer, and participating in the functions of a local church are vital to the Christian life. Since I trusted in Christ, I have made it my habit to read the Bible daily, that God may speak to me. I spend time with Him in prayer and seek the fellowship of others who belong to Him.

If you can answer Yes to these questions, you have great reason to rejoice. If there are some you cannot honestly answer with a Yes, don't lay this study book aside until you have allowed God to deal with you about them.